GOD, SCIENCE & EVOLUTION

GOD, SCIENCE & EVOLUTION

Prof. E H Andrews

EVANGELICAL PRESS,
16/18, High Street, Welwyn, Hertfordshire AL6 9EQ, England

© Evangelical Press 1980
First published 1980

ISBN 0 85234 146 6

Cover design by Peter Wagstaff.

Typeset in Great Britain by Solo Typesetting, Maidstone.

Printed in U.S.A.

Contents

Introduction

Chapter

Introduction

The divorce between science and religion is one of the most significant aspects of our modern philosophical scene. The unity of truth and knowledge, which has always been a prime objective of thinkers down the ages, has been all but abandoned by our Western culture. It has been replaced by a schizophrenic world-view which divorces the 'real' pragmatic world of science (the material universe) from the insubstantial thought-world in which philosophy and religious belief are permitted to function, like birds imprisoned in a cage of subjectivity. This dichotomy between our inner and outward lives is bound to introduce serious tensions on both the personal and social levels. The 'real' world of social intercourse and political decision is no longer regulated, as it once was, by considerations of a philosophical and religious character. Legislation and morality alike are guided by a doctrine of blind pragmatic convenience rather than by moral absolutes, however dimly perceived. We do not today mould our social and political institutions by reference to God's moral laws, or even to the nature of man as a being created in the image of God. All is empirical and the only guiding principle we recognize is the law of cause and effect.

It is quite unfair, of course, to blame this state of affairs upon 'science'. Rather, science has merely provided an excuse for the rejection of spiritual principles and a belief in the moral authority of God. The founders of modern science actually saw the new 'natural philosophy' as demonstrating the order and harmony of creation and thus the existence and power of God. Today these same scientific disciplines are used by many to urge the redundancy of the spiritual dimension and banish God from His own universe. The god of evolution has replaced the God of creation and revelation.

That this has been allowed to happen is the fault of religious leaders rather than of scientists. In our own 'Christian' society the churches have themselves largely rejected the concept of objective revelation and a belief in the authority of the Bible, in favour of pragmatism. They have tried to carry over the scientific method into theology, not realizing that empiricism, which is a proper basis for physical science, is entirely inappropriate in our approach to God. This is not to say that Christianity is not experimental. Indeed, it is. But, unlike the physical world, God cannot be known by a humanistic methodology which begins with ourselves and our unaided senses. His transcendent nature together with our human blindness to spiritual truth require God to make Himself known, that is, they necessitate revelation, a concept both unknown and inappropriate to scientific endeavour.

Other Christian leaders, while clinging to biblical authority, have erred by withdrawing from the real world of practical experience into subjectivism. By confining the gospel of Jesus Christ to the purely personal realm, they have inadvertently underwritten the very dichotomy between the natural and spiritual worlds upon which materialism thrives. Admittedly, Christianity *is* a personal issue, involving the reconciliation of the individual sinner to God through the death and resurrection of Christ. But it is *more* than a personal matter since it involves a unified world-view in which man, nature, society and God are set in their proper relationships to one another. Starved of this philosophical unity, the Christian message becomes emaciated and the individual believer is forced, by default, to accept an essentially humanistic and even materialistic interpretation of the 'real' or natural world in which he has to function day by day. The tension between his inner beliefs and his practical life can become well nigh unbearable and may lead to demoralization and tacit withdrawal from the warfare of faith.

Perhaps I have overdrawn the picture, but the problems described are undoubtedly genuine. It would seem, then, that those who are both scientists and Christians have a special responsibility to do all in their power to correct the mistakes that have been made in these matters. Negatively, they must expose and reject the misuse of science as a handmaid of materialistic philosophy. They must refute the claim that science demonstrates the irrelevance and subjectivity of religious faith. They must argue that materialistic and evolutionary world-views are just as much philosophies as are Christian and religious world-views, that science no more authenticates the one than the other. They must show that science of itself is incapable of providing a complete philosophy of life and being; indeed, that science can only be understood in terms of ultimately spiritual principles. Positively, they must present an alternative biblical philosophy of nature and man that is true to both science and revelation and that will enable ordinary men to appreciate the essential unity of truth, both religious and scientific. They must offer a framework of thought in which the glories of God and man (as His special creation and the object of redeeming love) may be appreciated and in which also the individual, sinner though he be, may discover a dignity, liberty and purpose which materialistic humanism denies him absolutely.

This book is offered as a modest contribution to the fulfilment of these responsibilities. A collection of lectures and essays is not, perhaps, the best means of doing this, since it runs the risk of being disjointed and incomplete. On the other hand, the lectures and writings reproduced here have proved helpful to the few who have received them and may therefore be of value to a wider audience.

The chapters have been arranged to give a progression, from statements of broad principles and options, to much more detailed arguments on the nature of science and creation and the interpretation of miracles and providence in an age of science. Next the question of theistic evolution is considered and rejected as a means of reconciling biblical teaching with a scientific view of origins. The positive alternatives are then brought forward once again. Finally, almost as a postscript, there is an essay on the age of the earth, a subject fundamental to the evolutionary world-view which is so totally inimical to the biblical outlook.

CHAPTER ONE

Human knowledge is growing so rapidly, especially in the fields of science and technology, that an integrated view or philosophy of life is increasingly difficult to maintain. Fragmentation typifies the current state of thought and outlook, even among those scientists, philosophers and theologians who are supposed to be leading us into a deeper understanding of the universe and of our own humanity.

In this chapter, which is a shortened version of the author's 1968 'Inaugural Lecture' as Professor of Materials at Queen Mary College (University of London), a plea is made for a return to a unified view of man and nature. The only satisfactory starting-point for such a world-view is, in the writer's opinion, the biblical concept of a personal God who created and sustains the universe, and who reveals Himself to those that seek. Although light-hearted in style, the lecture is serious in intent and sets the keynote for the weightier arguments that follow in the later chapters.

Man, materials and materialism

A few days ago I received the following letter from a friend, who occupies the Chair of Engineering Materials at another university: 'I regret I shall be unable to attend your inaugural lecture, but look forward to reading it. I should like to have chosen your title for my own lecture, but thought I should have run into over-deep waters had I done so. It will be fascinating to see how you tackle it.'

I am not sure whether, by this token, inaugural addresses should be classified as river, sea or ocean-going lectures respectively, according to the depth of the waters they aspire to cross, or whether the dangers of foundering are related in any way to those depths. I trust that I will not founder and that you who have done me the kindness of attending this occasion will, if not fascinated, be interested in what I have to say.

Some, less generously minded than my correspondent, may observe that by my title I have pre-empted the whole of history, social anthropology, science, technology, philosophy and religion, and may feel this to be a trifle ambitious, even for an inaugural lecture. I hasten to put your minds at rest, for my concern is simply to put our subject, the science of materials, in context – the context, that is, of the society to which we belong and of the lives we each live.

The phrase 'the two cultures' has passed into common parlance. I wonder if the phrase is sufficient, serious as its implications are, to describe the fragmentation of knowledge which already exists. Perhaps we already live in an intellectual multiculture. A few weeks ago I met that doyen of polymer chemistry, Arthur Tobolsky, in a San Francisco street. He recounted how he had recently shown a Shakespearean quotation to a number of staff and students at Princeton University. Predictably enough, only a minority of scientists recognized its source. He then showed it to a similar selection of non-scientists. Their rate of success was hardly better than that of the scientists. He commented, 'I don't know about the two-culture society; it's more of a no-culture society.'

If the problem of fragmentation resides entirely in the *size* of the body of knowledge accumulated by mankind, all we can do is to make this knowledge increasingly accessible by such means as the computerization of information retrieval, and hope for the best. But I want to analyse the problem at a rather deeper level, because I think it has a deeper underlying cause — the absence of any substratum or philosophy to which localized areas of knowledge may be related; the absence of a world-view in terms of which our particular field of knowledge and, indeed, our own personal lives take on significance. It has always seemed to me that the elegance and genius of science lay in its ability to unify superficially unrelated phenomena, and I shall always remember the excitement I felt when, as an undergraduate, I learned how space and time could be treated in a unified manner in, for example, general relativity or electromagnetic theory. The history of science bears record, of course, to the dangers of overgeneralization, the tendency to go beyond what is proven in an attempt to express everything in terms of some simple universal principle, but the dangers implicit in generalization should not discourage us from seeking a proper 'world-view'. The pitfalls do, however, suggest that this world-view or philosophy of nature, to which our scientific and other knowledge is to be related, is not to be deduced from the body of scientific knowledge itself, with its changing fashions and notorious fallibility. In the closing part of my talk I want to explain my own views upon this matter.

Man and his materials

Technology is the backcloth of human life on the material plane. This has been true of human society down the centuries, for every tool or device invented for the safety, survival, subsistence, comfort or pleasure of man is an expression of technology, however primitive. The ox-cart and mud hut are as much the products of technology as are the jet aircraft and air-conditioned laboratory. It is by technology that man betters his adaptation to the environment and his powers over it; it is, more soberly, by technology that man has at the same time exposed himself to the possibilities of self-destruction on such a scale that, perhaps for the first time in human history, we have real reason to fear the very powers we have unleashed. However, for good or ill, like time itself, technology moves forward, for it is a self-generating activity. We cannot, nor should we desire to, arrest its motion; but its control is a matter of vital concern.

As technology is fundamental to civilization, so materials are fundamental to technology. Without materials there would be no technology, for materials are the essential link between inventions and ideas and the products of technological effort. They are the media by which ideas are realized, by which the innovator's dreams become tangible. They stand between the blueprint and the hardware, and, by the same token, set limits upon the achievement of ideas. Materials set the boundary conditions to technology and thus, indirectly, to the material aspects of civilization. It is no accident that the major epochs of human society (as materials scientists are wont to point out) are demarcated by such terms as the Stone Age, the Bronze Age (from 4000 B.C.) and the Iron Age (from 2000 B.C.).

The role of materials in technology can be classified as follows. An invention or an idea for a new machine, device or process must first be reduced to realistic workable and attainable form — this is the process of design. Here attention must be given to certain basic principles. The student howler of three mutually intermeshing gear wheels, for example, must be avoided. Wheels must be able to turn, ships to float and bridges to sustain their own weight. Not least, the principles of design involve the choice of materials available for the job. It is no use designing a structure which requires beams to carry loads of a million pounds per square inch, because no material exists capable of bearing such forces. Nor may we build ships of sodium metal, for all its lightness, because it reacts with water; or bridges of glass, for all its potential strength, because of its proneness to brittle failure. Such are trivial examples, but the obvious often goes unremarked and needs to be pointed out from time to time. It is remarkable that so little effort has, until recently, been devoted to training engineering students in this aspect of design.

Technology can advance only as fast as the available materials will allow. Frequently, in the past, it has advanced more slowly, retarded by factors unrelated to materials, but indications are that now, in some areas, the engineer is waiting on the materials which will enable him to design for greater efficiency, economy and potentiality than is yet possible.

Materials science — the impure art

Our next question must be: 'What is materials science?' The pedigree of even the humblest engineering material is impressive. The geologist prospects for and discovers mineral deposits from which most of our materials derive; the mining engineer wins the crude mineral from its ancient habitat and the extraction metallurgist or refiner produces from it a more or less pure material. Pure substances, however, seldom make good engineering materials and the process technologist and chemical engineer blend, mix and alloy until the desired combination of properties is achieved. It may appear from this that materials science (the study of the relationship between properties and internal or microstructure) is redundant, serving as nothing but a gloss upon the time-honoured technology of materials. There is a humbling degree of truth in this, but fortunately for some of us, it is not the whole truth. The justification for materials science, as something more than an intellectual exercise, lies in the statement I made a moment ago — that few pure substances make good engineering materials. Pure metals, for example, are usually far too soft to be of use. Refractory substances are often far too brittle. Some pure materials are far too prone to oxidation, and so one could continue. Materials science could, in this light, be described as 'the impure art', for its *raison d'être* rests largely in the important modifications to properties brought about by the admixture of 'impurities' or foreign substances.

Improvements due to impurities usually involve the modification in some way or other of the physical microstructure of the material, so that it is really more accurate to speak of the effects of heterogeneity rather than impurity, since the latter manifests itself by giving rise to non-uniformity of structure on some scale. We all, I think, realize that concrete is stronger than mortar because it has a heterogeneous structure; similar heterogeneity can exist on a much finer scale right down to the atomic level, where foreign or impurity atoms, dispersed in the crystal lattice of a pure substance, can give rise to spectacular increases in hardness. An intermediate example is the incorporation of carbon black powder in synthetic rubber, which can transform a cheesy, friable pure material into a tough, resilient tyre-tread.

Another form of heterogeneity which is vitally important is the occurrence of regions of disorder in an otherwise ordered or crystalline solid. Dislocations are regions in which the order within a crystal is disturbed and the ability of such disorder regions to move through the crystal when forces are applied gives rise to the phenomenon of plastic deformation – a phenomenon which, for the user of materials, has both good and bad points. Grain boundaries, which inhibit plastic deformation at low temperatures but may enhance it at high temperatures, and vacancies are also examples of disorder.

Disorder is of primary concern in polymers, for these materials are composed of long chainlike molecules which become so tangled that the achievement of perfect order (crystallinity) is seldom possible. The plastics and rubbers so familiar in everyday life are therefore either wholly disordered, like perspex, polystyrene and PVC, or else semicrystalline, containing 10% to 80% disordered material.

It is the task of materials science to describe the structure of materials, at all levels down to the atomic scale, and then to say how the structure governs the properties of strength, hardness, corrosion resistance, electrical conductivity, or whatever else is of concern to the engineer and designer.

Materials and materialism

I suppose it is the 'ism' in my title which has excited most curiosity in anticipation and which to some represents 'deep

waters' rather than 'safe ground'. To me, however, its inclusion
was no 'gimmick' to excite interest, but rather a necessity if I
was to express satisfactorily my theme of materials in their
context. I spoke earlier of the need for all of us, and particularly for us scientists, to have a world-view or philosophical
substratum to which to relate our own areas of knowledge
and experience. If we have no such philosophy, our science
becomes nothing more than the handmaid of materialism, by
which I mean a belief in the ultimate importance of things.
For all its apparent piety, the sentiment that bigger and
better, or shinier or faster things make the world a better
place to live is arrant materialism. Of course, our agricultural
and medical colleagues have more cogent arguments, for their
service to mankind is obvious. But they are driven, implicitly
at least, to appeal to such non-scientific principles as the
sanctity of human life and thus directly illustrate my point
that a non-scientific (or, better, ascientific) philosophy is
required to explain and underwrite the value of the activities
in which they engage.

What is 'materialism'? I have already given one definition –
a belief in the ultimate importance of things. I want to quote
a more trenchant definition provided by St Paul in the first
chapter of Romans. Speaking of the ancient world, he writes
that they 'worshipped and served the creature more than the
Creator,' who is God. The word 'creature' can also be trans-
lated 'creation' and probably bears this primary meaning.
Now few of us today would admit to being 'materialists', the
term being currently out of fashion. Nor would we confess,
perhaps, to 'worshipping' anything or anyone. But if we
take worship in its basic sense of 'living for', I think we must
allow that many more people are materialists than would
appear at first sight. In fact we must admit that we all devote
ourselves to *something;* we either live for (that is, worship
or ascribe ultimate value to) our personal pleasure, however
subtly disguised, or ambition, which is the same thing by
another name, or else find *outside of ourselves* some object
worthy of our self-dedication. Whether we like the term or
not, this object is our god, and our world-view (however ill-
defined) is our religion. It seems to me that we each have but
three alternatives: to worship things because they bring us

pleasure, which is materialism; to worship mankind itself because we are involved and because we have a corporate desire to see our kind triumph over his limitations and errors, which is humanism; or to worship the Creator because both His nature and ours demand that we do so. I have much sympathy for the honest humanist, because I believe his objectives are worthy. I am equally convinced of his error, because he pins his faith in human nature or intellect (both demonstrably imperfect and fallible) and, like the materialist, he cannot see beyond the material creation — though the humanist at least worships life rather than the inanimate!

To me, however, there must be a ground of reality which lies *outside* the creation, and in terms of which creation, both in its scientific and general aspects, can be understood. St Paul again draws a clear distinction for us: 'We look not at the things which are seen, but at the things which are not seen: for the things which are seen are temporal; but the things which are not seen are eternal' (2 Corinthians 4:18). Even from a scientific viewpoint, this is a remarkable statement, for the unseen world of elementary particles is indeed 'eternal' in comparison with the ever-changing and decaying world of things. Paul, however, was referring to a world external to the creation on any level, yet a world which co-exists and interacts with the creation as we know it, for (and I bring you one final quotation from the New Testament) it is said of Christ: 'All things were created by him, and for him . . . and by him *all things consist*' (Colossians 1: 16-17).

In these brief words we see the Christian view of nature, of creation, indeed of science in all its aspects. It is not the view that God simply created the universe and left it to itself like some gigantic self-powered timepiece. In biblical terms God is not dead to our world and our experience, as recent theological obituaries seem to suggest. The view is rather that God is immanent in creation (though at the same time transcendent, being *other* than the creation), and that the laws of science are an expression of His immanence. He is not the 'God of the gaps', a convenient explanation of what we do not yet understand. If He were this, His expulsion from the universe would be just a matter of time and, unlike the Cheshire cat, He would vanish by stages leaving not even the grin behind. On the contrary, He is the ground of all experience, including that branch of experience we call science: 'For in him we live, and move, and have our being.'

In these days it may seem strange for a scientist to espouse the cause of Christ. I would therefore remind you of men more eminent than your present lecturer is ever likely to be, who in the past have held similar views — men like Johann Kepler, who is reported to have exclaimed, on discovering the laws of planetary motion, 'Oh God, I am thinking Thy thoughts after Thee,' or Isaac Newton who stated that his scientific work was directed to those discoveries 'that would most work with reasoning men to a belief in the Deity'. Michael Faraday, on his deathbed, was asked, 'Mr Faraday, what are your speculations now?' and replied, 'I have no *speculations* — I know that my Redeemer liveth' — a quotation, of course, from the book of Job.

If to this we are tempted to reply that these men, great scientists though they were, were in this matter simply children of their 'superstitious' age, we should remember that we, too, are children of our age — our materialistic age — replete perhaps with unrelated knowledge but, could it be, less well equipped with *wisdom,* which is a very different thing?

CHAPTER TWO

Thinking man has only a limited number of options open to him as he seeks to interpret the meaning of his existence and the nature of his origins. In this lecture, originally delivered at a division of Imperial Chemical Industries Limited, we examine in turn the distinctly evolutionary options, only to reject them on rational grounds. We then consider the biblical account of the origin, purpose and destiny of man. There one may discover a wholly satisfying explanation of these vital questions and, additionally, the need for a personal response.

What is man?

The psalmist, addressing himself to God, asks, 'What is man, that thou art mindful of him?' Most of us, at some time or another, repeat this question: 'What is man?' because it is only as we understand what man *is* that we really know how to address ourselves to life. Our ambitions, our interpretation of the world around us, our attitudes towards our fellow human beings — all these things are critically affected by what we believe about the essential nature of man.

What options are available to us? The four options which I am going to put to you encompass, in my view at least, the whole range of possibilities open to thinking man. There are two options which we may call evolutionary, and two which we may call theistic or creationist, and we shall look at these in turn.

The evolutionary options

The theory of evolution has been so popularized that I do not need to spend a great deal of time describing it. Yet those of you who are involved in scientific research will know that it is very easy to misrepresent science when attempts are made to popularize it. This has certainly happened in the popularization of the theory of evolution, and we must therefore be clear as to its claims and deficiencies.

Basically, the theory of evolution tells us that man has arisen by the operation of physical and chemical law alone — what I will call a blind process of evolution (that is, a process not dependent upon intelligence). This blind process, we are told, not only accounts for the rise of the human and animal species, but can be extrapolated back to the origin of life itself, by a process which is called chemical evolution.

Chemical evolution

It is not my purpose in this lecture to discuss chemical evolution, but I wish to comment briefly in passing. I heard a very able exposition of certain aspects of this theory when I shared the platform at a recent symposium in the USA with Professor Melvin Calvin, the Nobel Prize winner. He gave a fascinating lecture as to how certain of the chemicals which are essential to the life process might have arisen by purely natural causes in the dawn of history. But he admitted, as any scientist must admit, that we are very, very far indeed from demonstrating how any of the basic biological 'stuff of life' could have come into being by such natural combinations. We are just scratching at the surface of possibilities. The spontaneous synthesis of even the simplest protein or nucleic acid would represent a vast extrapolation of anything yet demonstrated in the laboratory or theoretically envisaged. Even if it were eventually shown that such molecules could be made from the kind of chemicals which *may* have existed in a primitive earth atmosphere, it would only emphasize the absolute necessity of the intelligent control of the synthesis by the chemist himself! As far as I am aware, no scientist claims that the chemical evolution of life is proven. The most that can be said is that certain *small* steps in such a process might plausibly be explained by known chemical reactions. The rest is pure speculation.

Biological evolution

I want to spend more of my time on the subject of organic or biological evolution, and to ask the question: 'Is this theory scientifically sound?' I want to indicate just some of the vast gaps of credibility, as well as knowledge, which exist in the theory of evolution. It is necessary to counteract the popular view that the whole thing is proven. On the contrary, speaking as a scientist, I believe that in another twenty-five years the theory of evolution, as we know it now, may well have been totally discredited, purely on scientific grounds. The enormous gaps in the theory are beginning to emerge — not, of course, in the popular versions of evolution, but in the writings of the scientists who are studying these matters at a fundamental level.

The theory of biological evolution begins with a common observation, namely that in any species of creature or plant there are continual variations. No human child is completely identical to its parent. No dog, no fish, no flower reproduces identically. This is a matter of common experience. It is also the first point where serious confusion arises, because changes from generation to generation can be produced by two quite distinct causes.

The first is the *redistribution* of the same genetic material. We can talk, if you like, about the 'gene pool' in a species. As members of that species interbreed, different genes in the chromosomes come into conjunction and produce certain characteristics in the offspring — blue eyes or brown eyes, different colours of skin, the height to which a person grows. These variations within a species are nothing to do with evolution. They follow from the basic laws of genetics which were spelled out so ably by Mendel in 1859, and they demonstrate the immense amount of variety that can arise within a species. No matter how long that process of variation goes on, however, it is always convergent. That is, it always leaves you with the same species, whether it be a dog, a fish, or a chrysanthemum. Almost infinite variations can occur by recombination of the same genetic material, as animal and plant breeders have demonstrated time and time again, but these variations can never give rise to a change of species. This has seldom been made clear in the popular writings on the theory of evolution.

The changes that *can* give rise, in principle, to a process of evolution are known as *mutations,* where the genetic material is actually transformed by some external agency or by an accident during cell division. Mutations may occur spontaneously or may be induced by radiation, chemical treatment or some other means. Mutations take the system outside the existing potentialities in the 'gene pool' of a species. Typical effects of mutation include deficiencies in certain body chemicals, such as the haemoglobin in our blood, deformities, and the inability to manufacture pigment. (Albinism is the result of such a mutation.) Such mutations have been studied in the laboratory and the rate at which they occur can be measured — although in nature they are very infrequent.

Mutations are almost invariably harmful, though some do appear neutral in their effects on the viability of the organism.

But, says the evolutionist, mutation *may,* on rare occasions, give rise to an advantageous feature in the animal or plant. When this occurs the advantaged member of the population survives longer and produces more offspring. Thus 'natural selection' chooses out advantaged members which eventually come to predominate and so the species moves forward. Well, in theory that can happen. I have no quarrel with the basic ideas of mutation and natural selection as mechanisms which operate in nature, but in all the work that has been done since Darwin wrote his *Origin of Species,* there has been no convincing evidence of any mutation that has produced long-term advantages for a species. It is an arguable point, but the rate at which such advantageous mutations occur per-suade many biologists that this is not a process which could have given rise to the development of species or different phyla (the major animal groupings) from the original 'germ of life'.

Let me just read one or two quotations, because this may put things more succinctly.

'For over half a century scientists at Columbia University have been studying the common fruit fly *(Drosophila),* with a view to observing or inducing changes by mutations in them. Flies have been raised in varying environments, differences in temperature, humidity and the like, treated with x-rays and nuclear radiation. There have been changes. But some of the changes have been fatal. Others have altered the colour or size of eyes, wings and bristle hairs. Certain scientists would affirm that new species have been formed. This depends heavily upon one's definition of species. Undoubtedly new types of fruit flies have been produced. But whether anything has been produced which approaches an organism that shows any major difference has been denied also. They are still fruit flies. It appears that breeding of new varieties within certain limits is easily possible. Even producing new giant strains of plants by doubling the chromosomes is feasible. But to form a new major type of organism just has not been done. If one sticks to history, and avoids prophecy in this matter, one sees that evolution by the addition of small mutations has not been demonstrated. Changes do not proceed towards a different type, they cluster around the type of the original organism.'[1]

The unconvincing character of mutation plus natural selection as a sufficient mechanism of evolution is half admitted even in the most confident assertions of evolutionists. Thus Dobzhansky writes, 'The occurrence of the evolution of life in the history of the earth is established about as well as events not witnessed by human observers can be . . . The most pressing problems of evolutionary biology seem, at present, to belong to two groups — those concerned with the mechanics of evolution and those dealing with the biological uniqueness of man.'[2]

This ardent champion of evolution is forced to admit that the mechanics or mechanism of evolution, which we have been considering in brief outline above, still present pressing problems. (This is no less true in 1980 than in 1958.)

Goldschmitz, of the University of California, a geneticist, writes, 'Nobody has produced even a species by the selection of micro-mutations. In the best known organisms, like *Drosophila,* innumerable mutants are known. If we were able to combine a thousand or more of such mutants in a single individual this still would have no resemblance whatsoever to any type known as a species in nature.'[3]

Writing in his introduction to a 1959 edition of Darwin's *Origin of Species,* W.R. Thompson says, 'There is a great divergence of opinion amongst biologists, not only about the causes of evolution but even about the actual process. This divergence exists because the evidence is unsatisfactory and does not permit any certain conclusions.'[4]

There are more fundamental objections to the Darwinian (or strictly, neo-Darwinian) mechanism of evolution by mutation and natural selection. In order to achieve advantageous changes there must have been a co-operative process which produced a number of compensating and reinforcing mutations at one and the same time. If we suggest, for example, that birds' feathers arose by evolution from reptiles' scales, we must postulate not one, but a very large number of mutations, involving not only the physical form, but the controlling muscles, the oil-secreting glands and so on. Yet the advantage of feathers over scales, that alone would enable natural selection to operate, could not emerge until the feather had progressed to the stage of having a different function from that of the scale. The likelihood of the many reinforcing mutations necessary to carry forward the transformation all occurring before the pressure of selection could operate is remote. Take, as another example, the long neck of the giraffe. This is often given as an example of evolution. The giraffe was advantaged by having a longer neck because it could then eat food higher up in times of drought and famine. But the long neck of the giraffe could not have evolved without corresponding (and in evolutionary terms, quite independent) changes in the vascular system. This is because the difference in blood pressure between the 'head up' and 'head down' position is so great that the brain could not tolerate it without the very intricate system of valves which prevents this being a problem. It is no use just evolving a long neck. At the same time you have to evolve the appropriate anatomy and physiology to enable that long neck to give advantage to the animal. The chances of this happening by the coincidence of random mutations (in the various genes responsible for these different features of the animal) are incredibly small. On a more general note, one might also ask why *all* antelopes and related creatures did not evolve long necks if they were of such selective value to one species, and why were baby giraffes not selected out for extinction on account of their short stature?

The first problem, then, is that the evolutionary hypothesis of vast change occurring by small mutations is quite inadequate to account for even relatively minor differentiations within species, let alone the development of entirely new ones.

The fossil record

The main building block of the theory of evolution, the fossil record, proves anything but the validity of that theory. Let me quote from a Professor Vialleton, a Frenchman, writing as long ago as 1924: 'There is, then, when one considers evolution in the light of the real evidence, both great doubt and also exaggeration of its value, resulting in the idea that is very anthropomorphic, namely that everything has always begun very humbly and later has developed into very complex and lofty forms. Once again, one must say that this is not the picture presented by nature. One scarcely sees, throughout the geological ages, a gradual, slow multiplication of types of organisation. One does not at first find a unicellular being, then simple colonies of cells, then cellanturates, etc. On the contrary, Louis Agassiz remarked a long time ago in 1859, that in the first known fossils one finds, side by side, representatives of all the great groups, except the vertebrates, which seems to prove that the living world from its origin has been composed of diverse types, perfectly distinct one from the other, which have divided amongst themselves the various functions of life. Evolution has not begun from forms. truly simple in order to pass over into more complicated forms. The types of organisation one finds have always displayed their essential character initially. Genuine evolution, therefore, as one ascends the geological column from the first to the last representatives of any type of organisation, is trivial in sum and scarcely permits one to believe in the overweening power to effect biological transformation.'[5]

One could multiply this kind of quotation. Coulter, a biologist, tells us that the construction of a family tree is troublesome because of the missing links. He writes (my italics), 'Botanists construct as best they can an *imaginary* picture of the missing link so as to complete the sequence of steps in the evolution of the plant kingdom. Obviously such a practice is mainly *guesswork,* but like so many hypotheses has been very useful in organising subject matter and stimulating research. The record of the rocks reveals practically *nothing* of the earlier chapters in the evolution of the plant kingdom. For these, therefore, we must rely on types of plants still in existence plus a liberal measure of scientific *imagination.*'[6]

It is as you read this kind of quotation from the protagonists of evolution that you begin to think, 'What substance is there in the theory?' The embarrassment is that in the early days of the evolutionary theory much appeal was made to the incompleteness of the geological record. The links were missing. The expected transitional forms were absent but this could always be blamed on a lack of information; the fossil record was incomplete. But the argument has worn increasingly thin with the passing years. The biological record is so infinitely varied, the number of fossils and remains so fantastic, that if there *were* transitional forms they would most certainly have turned up. There are, of course, forms which are unknown today, and some of these *may* have been transitional, but the number of such examples is very small, and who is to say that a given fossil was transitional and not simply another distinct species which died out? Indeed, evolutionary relationships between fossil forms (or living ones for that matter) can only be inferred if one first assumes that evolution took place. For example, the celebrated series of horses, which is often claimed as final proof of evolution, are simply remains that have been arranged in ascending order of size on the assumption that they are related by evolutionary succession!

In the writer's view, the fossil record now constitutes a severe embarrassment to the theory of evolution and some biologists, recognizing this, are beginning to talk about a multiplicity of evolutionary trees, that is, they suppose that the basic groups of creatures arose from separate origins. This is a current theory and shows the desperate straits into which the original theory has fallen.

Evolutionary philosophy

I said at the beginning of this chapter that there were two evolutionary alternatives. Both of these have the same common origin which I have discussed already. In what way, then, do they differ?

If one believes that man is a piece of cosmic driftwood thrown up on the beach of time by a blind process of evolution, then rationally there is no meaning to life. Man is just an accident. There is no such thing as destiny, meaning or significance. One is forced into an existentialist philosophy: 'There is no meaning to our existence; eat, drink and be merry, for tomorrow we die.' This is the position at which many people have arrived.

But to the majority of thinking people this nihilistic

approach is intolerable. We just feel that there must be meaning, that it must matter whether I exist or do not exist, that mankind is not just a cosmic joke. The nihilistic and strictly logical attitude is not only very unwelcome, but unacceptable to the majority of men.

So we are led to our other evolutionary alternative. Beginning with the meaningless, blind process, a group of people, whose ideas are best known under the title 'scientific humanism' say, 'Now we have reached this point, we refuse to give up and say the whole thing is meaningless. We must take advantage of this evolutionary accident we call mankind and forge for ourselves a destiny to which man can aspire.'

Now this is a very noble viewpoint and one must respect the intellectual calibre of the people who subscribe to it. Here is no nihilism. Here is a willingness to accept the challenge. But I personally must reject this alternative for one basic reason — it puts far too much confidence in human nature. The only political group who tried deliberately to do what the scientific humanists tell us we should do were the Nazis in Germany, and they subscribed very fully to this opinion. You might also put certain contemporary racialist groups into this category, who keep alive the immoral dream of a race of men superior to their fellows.

Scientific humanists would throw up their hands in horror at the examples I have chosen. This destiny of man, they would protest, must be shaped by wise men, good and true. But their very evolutionary philosophy makes it difficult to define what you mean by wise, good and true, because it affords no ultimate or absolute moral values. Moral values, in their view, have just arisen in the course of history; they have no absolute significance. My definition of who is wise and what is good may differ from yours, it may differ from Huxley's and Haldane's and it certainly differs from Adolf Hitler's. The problem is: who is to decide? Who is to take control? Can any intellectual élite be trusted to remain incorrupt? And even if we did find somebody whom everybody trusted, how capable is man of creating his own destiny, and then steering his ship safely home to it? We have only to look around the world today and down the recent history of man to find that, with all his education, knowledge, science, ability and powers, man inspires little confidence as the arbiter of his own destiny.

Creationist options

Theistic evolution

The two alternatives discussed so far I have called evolutionary: the nihilistic, which leads to existentialism, and the scientific humanist view, which leads to an undue reliance upon the human intellect and human nature. Both, surely, are blind alleys in our search for meaning in life and existence.

The third alternative, to which we now come, still retains the theory of evolution but sees it as a controlled or purposive evolution. I am going to shovel a lot of different philosophies into this particular sack! It covers an enormous range of possibilities, from a conventional Christian viewpoint, which believes in a personal Creator who used the process of evolution to effect creation, to the mystical philosophies perhaps characterized by the Bergsonian concept of the *élan vital,* the life force, in which the very process of evolution is endowed with a mystical, spiritual quality. It also includes the approach of Teilhard de Chardin, who generalized evolution from the biological realm onward into an evolution of consciousness, mind, society and finally spirit. This is a teleological theory, looking forward to a goal, a peak to which man is climbing. That peak of attainment, that total spiritual consciousness, de Chardin refers to as God.

All of these approaches have in common the retention of biological evolution. At the same time they avoid the philosophical dilemmas of the pure evolutionist, and retain the idea of God, or at least the concept of the spiritual.

I reject this also, first of all because it is building upon the foundation of biological evolution, which I believe is not scientifically sound; and secondly, as long as biological evolution is retained, the spiritual dimension is just like icing on the cake. Let me explain what I mean by this. There is a basic philosophical principle derived from Occam's Razor that forbids any explanation of a phenomenon that is more complicated than it needs to be. If the evolutionary theory is adequate to explain the observed phenomena, namely the physical universe, why do you need to introduce concepts such as 'the spiritual' or God? This is a very difficult question to answer.

A third most fundamental objection to theistic evolution is that although it appears to reconcile the evolutionary theory and religion it does so at a great cost, sacrificing some of the basic insights of the Christian faith. I believe, for example, there is a basic conflict between the teachings of Scripture and theistic evolution and this theme is developed in detail in chapter 5.

The creationist view

Why is the theory of evolution such a popular theory? Why has not Einstein's theory of relativity or Maxwell's electromagnetic theory attained the same degree of popularity? Why is our fourth and final option, which is a thorough-going creationist viewpoint, so unacceptable to the mind of modern man?

I would suggest that evolutionary theory provides a kind of escape route for the human mind. There is something rather uncomfortable and inconvenient to the human heart about the concept of God. Once you admit that God, a personal supreme Being of some kind, created the heavens and the earth and that such a personality also created the human race, you immediately admit a relationship with that personality — the relationship of creature to a Creator, and that relationship automatically involves the idea of accountability. If I am a creature from the Creator's hand, by whatever route, then I am in some way accountable to Him. The first chapter of Romans says that men 'did not like to retain God in their knowledge'. There was something uncongenial about the idea of God and inference of accountability. Somehow I have to answer to God, to my Creator, for the way in which I have used my life.

These thoughts are difficult for the human heart to accept. The Bible puts it even more strongly. It says, 'The carnal [that is, natural] mind is enmity against God' (Romans 8:7). The natural mind is not only uncomfortable at the idea of accountability, but is positively rebellious against it. So a theory which enables us to dismiss God from the universe is a very acceptable and very comforting theory. I believe that this accounts for both the widespread popularity of evolution and the emotional tenacity with which it is normally embraced.

But evolution does not really solve the problem. If God did not create man and he evolved instead by processes of biological evolution following chemical evolution, stellar evolution, back to the primeval clouds of hydrogen, where did the hydrogen come from? 'Well,' you might say, 'it could have all been energy before it was matter.' Where then did the energy come from? You will see that sooner or later you reach a full stop. Now you may say, 'All right, we admit to having no explanation of ultimate origins, but there is no particular advantage in adding one more step and saying God created the energy or the matter, because then you ask "Where did God come from?" and you are no closer to an answer.' Let us accept for a moment that the idea of God may not help you at that point, but it does not hinder you either!

To me it is just as respectable, scientifically and intellectually, to claim that God created matter and energy, as it is to say that either matter and energy were always there, or simply to say we do not know where they came from. It is no more intellectually respectable to say that there is a process of continuous creation going on which we cannot study in the laboratory or know anything about, to admit a process totally unknown to science which 'must be going on because otherwise the alternative is God'. It is no more rational or objective to say *that* than to say, 'In the beginning God created the heaven and the earth.'

However, there are other advantages about the concept of God, and very profound advantages. For example, the theory of evolution takes for granted the existence and nature not only of matter and energy, but also of physical law. It does not ask about the nature or origin of the very laws of physics and chemistry to which it appeals. Why are there four quite different laws of force: gravitational, electromagnetic and the forces that hold the nucleus together, the 'weak' and 'strong' interactions? Why four, why not five, why not one? Science cannot answer that kind of question. The idea of God is a very satisfying hypothesis at this point. Not only do we identify God as the first cause and prime mover, the Creator, but we see Him throughout the universe as the sustainer and upholder of all things! There are two verses in the New Testament I would like to quote here. One says of Christ that He '[upholds] all things by the word of his power' (Hebrews 1:3). The other, in Colossians 1:17, says, 'By him all things consist.' These verses state that the integrity of the physical universe as we know it, the laws by which it operates, can be equated to 'the word of His power'. The laws of science are a present-tense moment-by-moment manifestation of the existence and will of God. If God were to pass out of existence in a moment, then the universe and all the laws of physics and chemistry would pass out of existence at that same moment. That is what the New Testament teaches and to me as a scientist it is an extremely satisfying hypothesis. To me as a Christian it is more than a hypothesis.

It leaves us with both a Creator and an ever-present cause for the whole of existence. Moreover, it takes the miraculous out of the realm of fantasy. If the operation of scientific law, of gravitational law, of electromagnetic law and so on, is simply the moment-by-moment 'upholding of all things' by the word of God's power, then the suspension of those laws, or the introduction of some temporary new law which we may class as miraculous, is no more difficult to explain than the existence of physical law itself. They are both of the same kind. They are both the moment-by-moment will of an immanent and almighty God. We shall develop these ideas at greater length in chapters 3 and 4.

Conclusion

It has not been my purpose simply to attack the theory of evolution. I believe it needs to be attacked, if only because the popular impression is given that evolution is scientifically proven. This view is terribly biased and ignores the yawning chasms in the theory which make it unacceptable to me as a scientist. I was also anxious, however, to present something positive. The Bible is not on the defensive against the theory of evolution, but has a positive theory of being to propose to us. It accounts for the creation and the sustenance of the physical universe, whereas evolution, even if accepted and admitted, only tells half the story, since it cannot account for the existence of the very physical law upon which it leans so heavily. The concept of creation and a sustaining God is to me far more satisfying as a cosmic theory than anything the theory of evolution has yet produced.

Beyond all the scientific and philosophical arguments, however, lies the personal issue with which I began this chapter. If we follow evolutionary options in answering the question: 'What is man?', we reject all that is meaningful in life. We reject all hopes of heaven, all belief that the universe is ultimately rational. If, on the other hand, we see in nature the eternal power of God, we are led back to the concept of man's accountability to his Creator. The questions of moral accountability and sin arise, and we begin to see that the Christian doctrines of creation and redemption from sin are inseparably linked together. The mission of Christ was to 'seek and to save that which was lost' (Luke 19:19), namely human beings like you and me. Here, then, is an option which not only proves to satisfy our questing minds, but comes to grips with our moral weaknesses and failures. It leads us not only to a unity of comprehension, but into personal contact with a forgiving God. Christ is not only the One who created all things (John 1:1-3), but the Saviour by whom we ourselves may be created anew, for 'If any man be in Christ, he is a new creature: old things are passed away; behold, all things are become new' (2 Corinthians 5:17).

References

1. Laird Harris, R., *Man; God's eternal creation*, Moody Press, Chicago, 1971, p.33.
2. Dobzhansky, T., 'Evolution at work', *Science*, vol.127, 1958, p.1092.
3. Goldschmitz, R.B., 'Evolution as viewed by one scientist', *American Scientist*, vol.40, 1952, p.94.
4. Thompson, W.R., Introduction to *Origin of Species*, Everyman's Library No.811, 1956, p.xii.
5. Shute, E., *Flaws in the theory of evolution*, Craig Press, Nutley, N. Jersey, 1961.
6. Newman, H.H., (ed.), *The nature of the world and of man*, Garden City Press, New York, p.321.

CHAPTER THREE

Is it possible for an ancient book such as the Bible to provide the Christian of today with a philosophy of modern science? The answer given to this question in the two chapters that follow is a resounding 'Yes.' A biblical view of science is not only possible, but essential, if the church is to refute effectively the largely materialistic outlook of our present age, an outlook that falsely claims the support of scientific evidence and knowledge. Without such a 'theology of science' we are unable to relate spiritual truth to the scientific view of nature and thus by default we allow atheism to claim science as its own. To the ordinary man, science represents the objective truth about the real world in which he lives. Layman though he be, he therefore tends to accept whatever world-view appears to command scientific respectability.

Chapters 3 and 4 set out the guidelines for a 'theology of science' which permits a biblical interpretation of science and all it reveals to us about the universe of which we are part. Originally given at the 1979 Annual Conference of the British Evangelical Council at Westminster Chapel, London, these lectures deal, firstly, with the idea of God as the universal Creator and Sustainer and, secondly, (in chapter 4) with the questions of miracle and divine providence in the physical world.

God in creation

The middle ground

I want you to imagine two mountains with a plain or valley between them. The first mountain represents biblical theology and world-view, while the second represents agnostic, atheistic or materialistic philosophy. What I shall term the 'middle ground' between them represents the physical universe in which we live out our daily existence.

This middle ground is disputed territory. There is a battle for its possession. Why should this be? Because a world-view which fails to encompass and account for the 'real' world around us is unlikely to capture the attention and allegiance of the minds of men. Whichever philosophy seems best to explain the physical context of human life is most likely to command man's sympathies, for it is in the natural world that he perceives himself to 'live and move and have his being'. Of course, the Christian understands that it is in God that we 'live and move and have our being', but the one who does not believe does not yet possess this insight. Yet it is to such people that the gospel of Jesus Christ is proclaimed and it is vital therefore that a biblical philosophy of nature should form an integral part of that gospel. The apostle John recognized this clearly in introducing his account of the life and work of Christ with a prologue which announces Christ as the 'Logos', the Creator of all things (John 1:1-3). We must therefore possess the middle ground in the sense that we offer a full and satisfying account of the physical universe (and of the science which so successfully describes it) in terms which are consistent with the biblical revelation. Otherwise that ground will be so overrun by materialistic philosophies, such as the evolutionary world-view, that men's minds will be wholly closed to the importance of spiritual things.

We face a situation, I fear, in which Christianity has largely yielded the middle ground to its opponents in the battle for the minds of men. We have allowed currency to the belief that the physical universe and science are no concern of religion. We have implied that what is material is not spiritual and is therefore quite irrelevant to the Christian message of personal salvation. I want to say, with all the emphasis I can, that this is a very dangerous and unbiblical attitude to adopt. For if we are to reach men and women with the gospel, we must do so in the context of their real-life experience. Among other things, this means that we must take account of our present scientific culture if we are effectively to evangelize.

In yielding this middle ground to the atheistic and agnostic philosophies of our day, we have failed to develop a true biblical theology of science and nature. Instead we have espoused a simplistic 'complementarity' in which we have said, 'The scientific description of the universe is valid and complete and self-contained, but, of course, you must also have a complementary theological description.' We have hidden, if you like, behind this concept of complementarity, whether consciously or not, to avoid the necessity of forging a truly biblical account of science and nature. It has been a position of strategic withdrawal by which we escaped involvement in the conflicts between science and religion.

I am sometimes accused of being too hard on the principle of complementarity and those who espouse it. I want to say that there is a measure of validity in the concept, but I think its dangers greatly outweigh its benefits. For what it does, at least in the eyes of the world around us, is to concede a materialistic view of the universe and of nature. We protest that men must also embrace the complementary theological view but they say, 'No, thank you very much, we are quite satisfied with the materialistic view. You are free to super-impose your theologies but we are satisfied with the self-contained naturalistic view of the universe which excludes God.' Thus I say that the middle ground is vital. We shall not reach men's minds unless we can offer an interpretation of the real world in which they find themselves. This is why I say we cannot evangelize effectively in our modern culture without a biblical theology of science. We must have something to say about the nature of science and its interpretation of the natural world in which we live that demonstrates the *necessity* of a higher theological level of understanding.

Creatio ex nihilo

'But,' you say, 'where do we start? What is the starting-point in developing this theology of science?' Well, the starting-point is really self-evident. We must start at the beginning and I want to suggest that the doctrine of *creatio ex nihilo* is the key to this whole subject. There is a tendency, I think, to take this familiar doctrine for granted and to consider it so self-evident that having defined it there is really nothing more to say. If someone attempted to preach a sermon on the doctrine of creation *ex nihilo* we might well fear that after five minutes he would have said all that could be said. To think in this way is seriously to underrate and underestimate the power of this particular doctrine, as I hope to show.

This is a neglected doctrine. I cannot remember ever hearing a sermon or an address or even reading a book about the subject. Which is rather strange, because this doctrine is absolutely basic to any attempt to provide a biblical view of science and the world around us. It is a neglected doctrine, and like the key that lay in Pilgrim's pocket all the time he languished in the dungeons of Doubting Castle, I believe we have here a key which will allow Christians to come off the defensive and take the offensive in this battle for the middle ground. It is a neglected doctrine and yet it underwrites the whole relationship between God and creation. This concept of the origin of the physical universe is the basis of all subsequent events and all subsequent relationships between God and His creation, including ourselves as human beings. To particularize this a little more, let me say that negatively the doctrine emphasizes the limitations of science, and positively it underlies a biblical concept of science. These are the two things that we are going to look at in this essay. Furthermore, this doctrine legitimizes the miraculous, undergirds the idea of providence and even implies human responsibility, thus anticipating the gospel.

These other things we shall take up in the following chapter.

Let us first of all see the doctrine of creation from nothing, *creatio ex nihilo,* stated in the Scriptures. These references do not in any sense constitute an exhaustive list, nor am I concerned here to expound these texts but rather to cite them. We must start, of course, on the threshold of the book of Genesis. 'In the beginning God created the heaven and the earth.' Here is the clearest possible statement that there *was* a beginning. This was obviously a beginning of the physical universe, not the beginning of God, since He was the pre-existent One who effected this beginning. He originated the entirety of what we know as the universe, 'the heavens and the earth', not from some prior substance but in a pure creative act. There are some who would take this verse and water it down. They do not do so in order to avoid the implications of an *ex nihilo* creation, but rather to substantiate the gap theory in which an attempt is made to introduce into the Genesis story a sufficiently long time-span to allow for the processes of evolution. In so doing they attempt to translate this verse as a conditional clause, making it read something like this: 'In the beginning of the creation of the heavens and the earth the earth became without form and void.' The primary statement becomes that relating to the condition of the earth rather than the creation. This, of course, robs the verse of its primary impact and empties it of the creative content which I am ascribing to it. The writer is not a Hebrew scholar and does not pretend to understand in full the arguments against this. I believe, however, that it can be demonstrated very clearly both from a theological argument and from the very form of the language that the traditional rendering is the correct one. Furthermore, to render this verse as a conditional clause is to introduce a circumlocution which is totally foreign to the crisp, straightforward style of the remainder of the chapter.

However, of course, we are not limited to Genesis 1. We come to Hebrews 11 and the third verse: 'By faith we understand that the worlds were prepared by the word of God, so that what is seen was not made out of things which are visible' (NASV). Here is as clear a statement as we could wish of the doctrine of creation from nothing. We turn to the prologue of John's Gospel and we read that 'All things were made by him; and without him was not anything made that was made.' By definition I think that must be a statement of this same doctrine, for if there had been anything that pre-dated the physical universe as we know it, then it would have to be something that He had previously made and the process of argument only pushes the beginning back a little further in time. Revelation 4:11 declares, 'Thou art worthy, O Lord, to receive glory and honour and power: for thou hast created all things, and for thy pleasure [because of Thy will] they are [exist] and were created.' Psalm 104, though highly poetic, is in many respects a statement of this doctrine. One particular statement is that God has 'stretched out the heavens like a curtain'. Poetic indeed, but nevertheless it embraces a statement of truth which is of significance, I think, to those who understand something of modern cosmology. Finally, Nehemiah 9:6 states, 'Thou hast made heaven, the heaven of heavens with all their host, the earth, and all things that are therein . . . and thou preservest them all.'

So we have many Scriptures on which to base our exposition of this doctrine and I would like to see this done more vigorously than is usually the case. My purpose here, however, is not to expound Scripture, but to provide the philosophical framework in which that can properly and logically be done.

Let me put into modern parlance, into scientific terminology, just what this doctrine of *creatio ex nihilo* means. It means that by an act (or fiat) of pure spiritual power God brought into being both matter and energy, which together I will call the substance of the universe. He also brought into being space and time which, in scientific thinking, combine to form what is called the space-time metric, a four-dimensional continuum, to which all events and all existence in the universe are referred. Finally, in addition to these things, God brought into operation the laws and rules of the natural world which control both the substance of the universe and the space-time metric. It is an oversimplification to think of the *ex nihilo* creation simply as the creation of matter, as perhaps many of us do. We have to realize that the creation of all these other things was vitally and essentially involved: matter, energy, the space-time metric and natural law. It is inconceivable that matter and energy, space and time, could have been brought into being without those rules and laws by which these entities both exist and interact.

A little earlier I used a tautology, namely the expression 'pure spirit'. It would have been sufficient to say that God is spirit, but I added the word 'pure' to emphasize that it was spirit and spirit alone that gave birth to the material universe. This then is a statement in modern terms of the doctrine we discover in the Scriptures quoted earlier, and this doctrine is a powerful weapon in our battle for the 'middle ground'. I want to spend the remainder of this chapter justifying this statement in some detail.

The limitations of science

I said at the beginning of this chapter that the *ex nihilo* creation leads us, firstly, to an understanding of the limitations of science and, secondly, to a biblical concept of the nature of science. These are the two things we are going to look at now. I am going to present the limitations of science in a negative way (science cannot do this or that), but in doing so I am not really making negative statements. In pointing out the limitations of science I am emphasizing positively the essential role that the *ex nihilo* creation has to assume in our total scheme. When I say, therefore, that firstly science cannot explain origins, I imply the positive assertion that theology can explain them by means of the doctrine of creation.

The inability of science to explain *origins* is a direct consequence of the very nature of science, for it is the study of what 'is', namely, the physical universe as we find and observe it around us. Science cannot speculate about that which 'was'. I am not, of course, saying here that science cannot describe past events. It can indeed do so, but only in so far as those past events were controlled by the laws that are now known to operate, only as long as they took place in a world such as the one we observe today. It is perfectly proper for us to extrapolate our scientific knowledge backwards in time, as long as the rules do not change or undergo a discontinuity at some past moment. It is quite impossible, however, to extrapolate backwards in time beyond any juncture at which the laws of science underwent change. In particular, we cannot extrapolate back to a time when those laws did not exist.

The unbelieving world has been quick to recognize the implications of this problem. They have recognized the impossibility of explaining the origin of the basic stuff of the universe (matter, energy, space, time and law) in terms of present scientific processes. Attempts have been made, therefore, to avoid altogether the embarrassment of a beginning, and the best known of these attempts is probably the theory of continuous creation. This idea was advanced some thirty-five years ago by Bondi and Gold, and later developed by Hoyle and Narliker. The attraction of the idea lay clearly in its philosophical rather than its scientific content. Indeed the scientific content of this theory was such as to violate one of the most fundamental laws of science, namely the conservation of matter and energy. But the proponents of the theory, and those who still support it (although it is largely out of favour today), were willing to sacrifice the most cherished principles of science in order to gain their philosophical objectives, namely, to do away with the necessity for origins, to banish the idea of a beginning. Instead they would substitute a 'steady state' model in which there was no beginning and to which there is no ending of the universe. I say that this theory has been discredited, as indeed it has on purely scientific grounds. But I would warn you that the philosophical ambitions which promoted it are still alive. For example, in the context of the currently accepted 'big bang' theory of the origin of the universe, there is a variation of the steady state theory, namely, the idea that the universe may oscillate unendingly between explosion, expansion, collapse and re-birth in a fresh explosion. Let us not imagine, then, just because scientific evidence has ruled out the former theory of continuous creation, that our materialistic philosophers have abandoned their attempts to banish the idea of an ultimate origin of the universe.

Some of you may have read a book by this year's Nobel Prize winner, Steven Weinberg, entitled *The First Three*

Minutes. In it he describes the 'standard model' of the universe, in which the beginning is conceived to have consisted in an explosion of unimaginable magnitude occurring not in a single place but, as it were, uniformly throughout what then became space itself. The space-time metric in which the infant universe was contained was in all likelihood very different from that which we know today. The book then traces, by way of theoretical speculation, the development of that universe in terms of its content of matter and energy, its temperature and the processes which may have occurred, during the first three minutes of its existence. In actual fact, these ideas are pressed back to speculate on what happened within the first one-hundredth second of the existence of the universe. It may well be that some version of the 'big bang' theory is compatible with the biblical account of creation. I certainly do not rule that possibility out of court. But no matter how close to the instant of origin one may be able to press the scientific model of the cosmos, it remains impossible for such an explanation to be applied at or before the zero time point. Thus it follows that science, even at its most speculative, must of necessity stop short of offering any explanation or even description of the actual event of origin. It is at this point then that theology must enter the picture, not as an admission of defeat but rather on account of the very nature of science.

The second inherent limitation in science is its *inability* to explain *scientific law.* I have already suggested that the rules which govern and control the physical world are an implicit and inseparable part of the creation fiat. If this is so, it follows that scientific law can no more be explained by science than can the *ex nihilo* origin itself. Let me explain this in more detail. There is a certain arbitrariness about scientific law. For example, the law of gravity states that the gravitational force between two masses is proportional to the product of those masses divided by the square of the distance between them. It is quite conceivable that a universe could exist in which the gravitational force was proportional to the inverse cube of the distance, rather than the inverse square. Or, rather than the square or cube, it might even be the power 2.5 or 2.7, or some other non-integral figure. There is no reason that science can offer to explain why the law of gravity should be exactly what it is. There are an infinity of alternative laws that might have been. If, walking along a beach, I pick up a single pebble, I automatically reject in that very act a myriad other pebbles that might have been chosen instead. This is what God has, in effect, done in setting forth the laws of science. Each law, whether expressed in words or mathematical symbols, represents a choice from among an infinity of possibilities. Of course, if the laws were different, the universe in which we lived would itself be different, but provided the laws were not mutually exclusive or contradictory, that universe could exist.

If we ask science why the laws are such as they are, and not otherwise, if we ask why the law of gravity is an inverse square law with respect to distance, science can do nothing but shrug its mathematical shoulders and reply, 'That question lies outside my terms of reference.' Science must take the universe as it finds it, and this is one of its most profound limitations. The *ex nihilo* creation answers the question that science cannot. Why is the universe as it is? Simply because God chose that it should be so. His choice of one law over against the possible alternatives was a deliberate act which automatically excluded those other alternatives. Lest some should think that what I have just said is childishly simple, let me point out where lies the profundity of these statements. It lies in the fact that choice is an attribute or action of intelligence. Without intelligence there is no true choosing but only a response to the rules of chance. But before even *those* rules existed, a choice or distinction was made as to what they should be! The unavoidable conclusion is, therefore, that intelligence pre-existed the natural universe and the laws by which it functions. The only escape from this argument lies in a total agnosticism concerning the fundamental nature of scientific law.

There is one other important thing that needs to be said here, and which leads to the subject that will be dealt with in the following chapter of this book. If it is true that the whole physical universe derived from pure spirit, it follows that we have in our present age a coexistence of the material and the spiritual realms. It is inconceivable that the prime mover, the pure spirit, should in some way vanish or disappear from the scene once the material universe had been created. So it is a logical necessity of the *ex nihilo* creation that we have in our present time a coexistence of the material and spiritual.

From this we may move forward to another conclusion, namely, that the doctrine of *ex nihilo* creation leads naturally to what I will call the doctrine of 'universal sustenance'. I use this expression to indicate that the material universe is sustained by, and has a derivative existence from, the spiritual realm. We do not simply think of a coexistence of the two, but see a dependent relationship of the physical upon the spiritual. The apostle Paul said, 'We look not at the things which are seen, but at the things which are not seen: for the things which are seen are temporal; but the things which are not seen are eternal' (2 Corinthians 4:18).

Earlier this year I spent a few days in the northern part of Italy, on the shores of Lake Garda. There, on that very beautiful mountain lake, there are many places where the cliffs rise sheer from the waters for a thousand feet or more. The massive rock plunges from snow-capped peaks and disappears below the surface of the lake, to re-emerge, of course, on the far side. One could argue from the superficial appearance that the land simply stops when it reaches the lake surface, but we know that this is not the case. The rock, although it plunges beneath the water, is still *there.* So important is its presence that if there were no rock beneath the surface, there would be no water in the lake! This is a faint picture of what I am trying to say about the coexistence of the material and the spiritual realms. It is not merely coexistence; it is a supportive and sustaining relationship between the invisible and the visible realms. As the hidden rock that forms the lake bottom supports and contains the visible waters, so the hidden realm of pure spirit upholds the material universe to which it earlier gave birth. The material world only exists because it is undergirded by the spiritual world.

Finally in this section, I would suggest that science cannot explain *the phenomenon of mind.*

What is mind? Either mind is self-existent, and therefore non-material in origin, or else it is the emanation or by-product of the physical brain. It seems to me that there is no alternative to these options. Either mind is a consequence of the electrical impulses and organization of an anatomical organ, or else it is a self-existent phenomenon which 'rides upon' brain function without deriving from it. A well-known philosophical argument points out that if thought is merely a by-product of brain function, then our thoughts and ideas have no validity, since they are simply the consequence of non-rational physiological and chemical processes which are not themselves endued with 'meaning'. If this be the case, then these arguments are themselves meaningless and void of content and cannot be relied upon as 'true' in any sense. We are thus forced either to accept that mind has a genuine existence apart from brain function or else we are locked into a circular argument that empties all philosophy of meaning.

The concept of self-existent mind is perfectly respectable, not only because it is the position we adopt intuitively, nor even because the alternative makes nonsense, as we have just seen. It is increasingly recognized, on the basis of what is called 'information theory', that information and concept may 'ride' upon matter, while at the same time being something other than matter. To give a simple illustration, I might take a number of symbols from our alphabet and set them down on paper. They may make sense or nonsense according to the way they are arranged. If I write down, say, three hundred such symbols, even if they are arranged in a pattern, they may still convey no meaning. I could, however, arrange the same symbols into words and sentences to spell out a communication full of significance for the reader. It is obvious that the message and the meaning are quite independent of the symbols. The same message written in a foreign language will require different symbols. I might even invent a new language to express my message and provided that you were taught the conventions of that language, you could read and understand what I was saying. Thus although the message has no manifest existence apart from the symbols (it 'rides' upon the symbols), it is clear that the symbols themselves do not equate with the meaning they convey. The symbols are arbitrary and may (by agreement between the writer and the reader) be varied without affecting the meaning. So, by analogy, we may logically claim that mind has an existence independent of brain function, just as a message has an existence independent of the physical symbolism used to convey it. In physical terms you cannot separate the message from the symbols, of course, and, similarly, mind and brain cannot be separated. But our inability to effect physical separation in no way contradicts the claim that mind has an independent existence in the world of spiritual, non-physical reality.

Even from a scientific viewpoint, then, it is quite proper to assert the independent reality of mind, and this assertion is a logical requirement of the doctrine of *ex nihilo* creation. For pure spirit *is* mind, since it is impossible to conceive of spirit apart from the idea of mind. This is not to say that pure spirit is limited to mind but it must clearly possess a 'mental' dimension. Pure spirit is not form. It is not motion. It is not material. It must be perceived as intelligent or it must remain altogether incomprehensible to us. It should not surprise us therefore that, as creatures in the material universe, we can nevertheless identify a category of non-material existence that we call mind. It is a natural and inevitable consequence of the *ex nihilo* creation and of the interaction between the material and spiritual realms inexorably associated with such an origin.

Going further, it follows naturally that the physical universe as we find it is capable of being codified and understood in terms of mental concepts, including such things as mathematics and scientific law, for this material world, like our own human minds, derives from the mind of God. The compatibility between our minds and the character of the created world (which alone permits that world to be described in rational scientific terms) is evidence that both human mind and nature flow from the same source, namely the eternal pre-existent mind that we call God.

The nature of science

So much for the limitations of science. Let us now turn to consider the nature of science. I want to suggest five propositions which are descriptive of science. I will set them down and then examine the impact upon them of the doctrine of *ex nihilo* creation.

1. Firstly, science is *law*. The laws that govern both the sub-stance and the processes of nature can be comprehended in a single word, 'interaction'. That is to say, the laws of science describe the manner in which matter and energy interact to produce the phenomenon we call the universe. 'Science' is, of course, something of a portmanteau word, but in essence science, both in its pursuit and as a body of knowledge, can be reduced to the study of these interactions. The corpus of scientific knowledge can therefore be expressed as a collection of laws, while the endless search of the scientist is for unity within the diversity of laws that describe the way nature behaves. The high object of science is to reduce our under-standing of the universe to ever more fundamental principles, from which the great variety of interactions may be derived as so many special cases. This is illustrated by the 1979 Nobel Prize for physics awarded to two men who demonstrated that, at sufficiently high temperatures, two of the four known laws of force in nature merge into a single law. There is, then, a continual search for simplicity, a desire to reduce the plethora of different laws to a few basic general principles. The further this search is rewarded by success, the more truly can it be asserted that science *is* law.

2. Secondly, science is *derivative from law*. That is, what we know as science is a consequence of law, and not its cause. This is an important distinction because it is easy to fall into the error of thinking that science somehow creates the laws of nature. This is not the case. Science simply discovers and describes the rules by which the universe operates, and is thus derivative. It is not that the laws have somehow come into existence as a consequence of scientific endeavour. Rather, it is because the world is, in a physical sense, law-abiding that it becomes possible for us to pursue the activity we call science. If the rules of nature changed from day to day, or if the behaviour of matter and energy fluctuated in a random and unpredictable manner, it would be impossible for science to exist.

3. Thirdly, science is *rational*. We have already anticipated this point by recognizing that the human mind, in its ration-ality, is alone equipped to practise science. The fact that we can express the laws that control the universe in terms that a

rational mind can formulate means that science and the underlying reality that it seeks to portray are both rational in character.

4. Fourthly, science is *unified*. We have already referred to the search for generality and basic principle, and this search is driven by the conviction among scientists that there exists an integrity in the universe, a harmony, a design. The world of nature is a single entity, controlled by mathematically expressible and interlocking processes. The universe is not, to the scientist, a rag-bag of fortuitous, meaningless and contradictory events. It is a system which exhibits a fundamental unity of structure and harmony of function. This alone justifies the pursuit of pure science.

5. Fifthly, science is *universal in space and time*. As far as we know, the laws of science are the same on earth, on the moon, in the sun and in the furthermost galaxies. The laws of yesterday are the same as the laws of today, and tomorrow's laws will be the same as today's. There is, in other words, a consistency in the structure and function of the universe, which is easy to take for granted, but which is not trivial in its implications.

The major point I want to make concerning the propositions is that science cannot find cause for these things within itself. These concepts, which describe the nature of science, do not arise from science itself and therefore must lie outside it. They are philosophical concepts for which science itself can offer no explanation and upon which science itself can throw no light. Far from 'explaining' the universe, science on its own begs all the essential questions about the nature of the physical world and, indeed, about its own nature. More generously, perhaps, we might say that science focusses attention on the necessity for a philosophical world-view, for, without such undergirding, science throws up more questions than it answers (specifically, *why* does science exhibit the characteristics outlined in my five propositions above?).

Universal sustenance

This leads us to the doctrine of 'universal sustenance' which, I maintain, provides just such a philosophical world-view and one which is derived wholly from the biblical record. The doctrine states that God not only created the universe at its origin, but that He actively, moment by moment, sustains the universe in all its manifestations, both in its substance and process. In particular, He does so in and through the scientific laws by which we choose to describe the world around us. (I realize that traditionally this idea would be considered part of the doctrine of providence, but I am deliberately separating this teaching from providence to bring it forward with greater clarity and force.)

This doctrine of universal sustenance is implied by the *ex nihilo* creation. This was the force of my illustration concerning the mountains of Lake Garda, namely that the coexistence of the spiritual and the material implies a dependence of the latter upon the former ('The things that are seen are temporal; but the things that are not seen are eternal'). This implication is greatly strengthened by a number of Scriptures. I like the Authorized Version translation of Revelation 4:11: 'For thy pleasure they [that is, all things] are and were created.' God has a purpose for this world and those who inhabit it, and just to state this is to grant that there must be a continual interaction between the material and spiritual realms. If God is to receive pleasure from His creation, He cannot be a remote and uninvolved figure. He must be active in the real world. But we do not need to rely upon inference to uphold the concept of universal sustenance, for the doctrine is plainly stated in the Bible. Colossians 1:17 states that 'He [Christ] is before all things, and by Him all things consist.' The verb 'is' here signifies 'exists' and the clause that contains it therefore has a temporal meaning rather than denoting supremacy (although 'before' may well carry the additional meaning of pre-eminence, seeing that the whole passage is concerned with just that issue). Paul almost always uses the Greek word *pro* in its temporal sense, although Luke does use it in the sense of pre-eminence. Our Scripture therefore states that Christ pre-existed the material and, indeed, the angelic creation and 'in Him' all created things hold together. Everything derives its being and integrity from the presence and activity of the Second Person of the Trinity. Earlier I said that all science can be reduced to law, and that law describes interaction. This interaction conveys just the same idea as the word 'consists', so that we may claim direct scriptural authority for the view that the entire physical world derives its being and behaviour from the present-tense activity of the triune God. The second reference I want to quote is Hebrews 1:3, where we read that Christ 'upholds all things by the word of his power'. Just as the natural universe could be said to rest upon a framework of natural law, so equally it can be said to be upheld by the word of Christ's power. Thus we may actually equate natural law (or rather the reality or principle that it imperfectly describes) with the word of divine power. We see again that the Bible explains something that science itself is not capable of explaining, namely the fundamental nature of scientific law. These laws of nature are none other than the direct commands of God, the instantaneous word of power that emanates from the creator Spirit, who alone is self-existent. A third Scripture that is germane to our subject is Acts 17:28: 'For in him we live, and move, and have our being.' The living and the moving are redolent of process, the processes of the natural world which is the sphere of scientific investigation. These natural processes, then, operate 'in Him', echoing the same truth as we have already emphasized, namely that the existence of God and the spiritual realm is fundamental to the physical universe. In the clause that follows: 'In Him we . . . have our being', it is not so much process that is represented, as existence itself. The very substance of created things is here attributed to the sustenance of God. Thus, both in its substance and its process, the material universe is derivative from the being and intent of God.

What we are doing here is to re-enunciate the idea of the immanence of God, a belief that Christians have always held. God is present in nature, though not to be equated with nature as the pantheist would maintain. God is not nature; He transcends nature, and the physical world is not part of God but merely His handiwork. Nevertheless we must avoid the opposite error from pantheism, namely, the mistake of placing God completely outside of His creation so that the latter becomes no more than a machine, having an existence independent of God. God is transcendent, but He is also immanent, present, at hand in His creation, for 'in Him we live, and move, and have our being'. But we have gone even further than to say that God is present in nature. We have claimed scriptural authority for the view that God's presence is a sustaining presence. The physical universe in all its manifestations exists because God wills it to exist, moment by moment. It is not a self-existent creation, but is upheld at every instant of time by the immediate word of His power. Applying these concepts, then, to our five principles we come to the following conclusions.

Firstly, scientific law has an underlying character, for it is the word of God's power. Secondly, the idea that science is derivative from law follows very naturally from the doctrine of universal sustenance. Science must be derivative because the creation that it studies is itself derivative from the spiritual realm. Thirdly, science is rational because the things it studies are the products of the mind of God and it is for this reason, and this reason only, that science is comprehensible to man and accessible to human reason at all. Fourthly, I said that science is unified, and we now see this as an inevitable consequence of the fact that the world is the product of a single purposive mind, the mind of God. It is not surprising, then, that we find, increasingly as our knowledge grows, that the laws and rules by which the universe operates are unified parts of a single grand design. Fifthly, we saw that within certain limits, science is universal. There is no *a priori* reason why this should be the case, but it is an immediate and natural deduction from our doctrine of the sustenance of God in nature. The universal and omnipresent Creator, sustaining the entire universe by the word of His power, bestows an intrinsic universality upon the processes of science. His rule is uniform throughout His vast domain.

Finally, the whole doctrine of the universal sustenance of God leads on to the more human, less philosophical concept of the immediacy of God. His immediacy in science has been the burden of this chapter; in the next we shall look at His immediacy in miracle and providence.

CHAPTER FOUR

Is God actively involved in nature and in history? The very expressions 'miracle' and 'providence' imply an affirmative answer. But how can miracles occur in a universe ruled by scientific law? How can the 'blind forces' of nature be manipulated by a non-physical Deity to bring about specific events in history and human experience? How can the spiritual realm interact with the physical world without introducing chaos in the latter? These are some of the questions tackled in this second address at the British Evangelical Council Conference in 1979.

Our task here is to show how the direct involvement of God with our 'real' world may be seen as a fitting and natural consequence of the relationship between God and His creation considered in chapter 3, rather than as an arbitrary meddling or, even worse, the superstitious invention of simple minds.

God in miracle and providence

The main theme of the previous chapter was the subject or doctrine of the *ex nihilo* creation, the idea that all the physical and visible universe sprang from the fiat of a God who is and was pure spirit. From that primary doctrine we derived the secondary doctrine of universal sustenance, that is, the idea that God upholds all things by the word of His power and that in Him, the Second Person of the Trinity, all things consist or hold together. We saw that this doctrine flows naturally from the concept of an *ex nihilo* creation, but that it is also separately and independently stated in Scripture. We looked at this doctrine of universal sustenance and saw that it provides a biblical view of the nature and character of science.

We now want to move on to see how the idea of universal sustenance legitimizes the concept of miracle, how it undergirds the doctrine of providence and how it points to the doctrine of human accountability (and thus prepares the way for the gospel). Previously, universal sustenance showed us the way to a biblical view of science. Now that same doctrine may help us see how miracles and providence can be understood in the context of a scientifically characterized universe.

Miracles

First of all then, let us consider the subject of miracles. At the outset let it be clear that the miraculous is absolutely fundamental to Christian theology and the gospel of Jesus Christ. There is no way that we can banish the miraculous from our gospel without sacrificing the gospel itself. The interaction of God and the spiritual realm with our material universe is fundamental because Christianity is based upon *historical* facts, the facts of the incarnation, the resurrection and indeed the future resurrection and judgement. All of these were, or will be, miraculous events. It has always seemed rather inconsistent to me that some Christians should do everything possible to avoid invoking the miraculous in the discussion of creation, because they must admit it in discussing the gospel.

On the other hand it is essential for us to have a proper theological approach to the miraculous, a theology of miracles. It is not sufficient for us merely to say that miracles happened because the Bible says so. The people to whom we are preaching in this scientific age demand a fuller explanation. Therefore my purpose is to examine the concept of miracles in the context of the scientific and materialistic culture in which we find ourselves.

Let me then define what I mean by a miracle. My definition is as follows: 'A miracle is an event consequent upon a localized change in the laws of nature.' You may recognize that this definition relates to what I wrote in chapter 3 about the character of scientific law as being something which has an immediately spiritual origin and cause, and which can be represented in biblical terms as 'the word of God's power'.

Let us look at this definition of miracles and see where it takes us. Firstly, it does exclude some biblical events which we normally and loosely refer to as miraculous. For example, the crossing of the Red Sea by the Israelites is plainly ascribed in Scripture to natural causes. There was a strong wind which forced back the waters and held them in place. There is no indication that we are dealing there with a miracle in the sense that I have defined it, namely an event requiring an alteration in the laws of nature. Because natural causes were employed (albeit by God Himself) this event falls under the heading of providence rather than miracle, as we shall see presently. Thus this definition of miracles is somewhat restrictive in relation to what I might call a 'popular' view. It is also clear, I think, that I am only concerned here with events in the material world and not those occurring solely within the spiritual realm, like the 'new birth', which we often refer to as miraculous since it is a direct work of the Spirit of God.

The second point to notice is that a miracle involves a change in natural law. This is an uncompromising statement, because it forbids any scientific 'explanation' of the miraculous. This follows because science is the study and codification of natural law, that is, those laws which habitually, normally and universally control the working of the world in which we live. If those natural laws are, for a time, changed then what happens during that period of change cannot be comprehended under the heading of 'science'. Science can make no comment whatsoever about events which are consequent upon a change in the laws of nature. You notice that I say 'a change' rather than a 'suspension' of the laws of nature. A suspension suggests a void, an absence of law. We are not, however, proposing an absence of law but rather the replacement of one set of laws by different ones.

Although our definition forbids any scientific account of miracles, it does not follow that science can in any way disprove miracles or demonstrate that they cannot happen. This is a common fallacy, to think that science states or implies that miracles cannot occur. The truth of the matter is, of course, that miracles lie outside of the terms of reference of science so that science can, in and of itself, make no contribution to an understanding of the miraculous. Remember that science does not create natural law. Rather the reverse is true, namely that natural law is the cause of, and justification for, science. It is because the laws exist that science can also exist. Science studies that which already exists in this universe and must concern itself with the habitual and universal behaviour exhibited by nature. It cannot consider any unusual or altered behaviour that may take place.

Having said this, let me state what should be obvious from the previous chapter, namely that the alteration of natural law that occurs when miracles happen is an intellectually acceptable idea. For if natural law is, as I have maintained, the moment-by-moment will of God, the instantaneous 'word of His power', then any change in the hierarchy of natural law is brought about by a momentary change in the 'instructions' that God 'issues' to His created universe. Because natural law is His immediate will, then a departure from that law must equally be His will for that moment of space and time. This is the key to the legitimization of the miraculous: namely, a proper understanding of the nature of scientific law allows us to say that the miraculous is just as natural, just as rational, as the normative laws of nature. Let me use an illustration which may help to clarify this point. I habitually travel from my home to my office in London by train. An observer, like the scientist observing the natural world, would quickly discover the rules or 'laws' which control my travelling habits. He would find that five days each week I leave my home and travel by train, then that I miss two days before recommencing the cycle. But very occasionally, twice a year perhaps, I find that I need a car in London and therefore travel by road instead of by rail. To the observer that would appear to be a breach or alteration in my 'laws' of travel. But although this is an infrequent occurrence, and therefore exceptional, my journey by car is no less a deliberate act of my will than is my habitual choice of train as a means of transport. Thus in the matter of God's control of the universe there is a natural and habitual control, designated in Scripture as the 'word of His power' and designated by science as natural law. But there is also an unusual, infrequent and limited exercise of the divine will in what we describe as miracle and in which the 'normal' is superseded by the 'special' in a deliberate act of God carried out for a particular reason. Miracles are thus just a different manifestation of the divine will from that which we regard as 'normal' in nature; but both nature and miracle share the common characteristic of being the will of God in moment-by-moment action.

Let us move on to the second aspect of my definition of the miraculous, namely that it involves a *localized* change in the laws of nature. It is self-evident that miracles are normally localized in space and time. (Even the *ex nihilo* creation itself was localized in time, if not in space.) At the wedding of Cana, it was only the water in the stone jars that turned into wine, not the contents of the local well. Nor did the water which constitutes so much of the human body change into wine in those who stood by. The results might have been interesting had it done so! When Mary conceived as a virgin, it was a unique event which did not involve parthenogenesis in all the unmarried women of Judaea. Miracles are thus demonstrably localized in space and time, and this does raise a possible problem concerning the explanation of miracles that I advanced earlier. The problem is this: if God's normal will, which we observe as natural law, is universal, how is it that any change in that law should be local? There is an asymmetry here in God's behaviour towards the universe. The 'word of His power' appears to be a universal operation. The laws are the same on earth, on Mars and, as far as we know, in the remotest galaxy. They were the same yesterday as they are today and will be tomorrow, whereas this change in natural law which we call miracle, is localized, introducing an asymmetry. Let it be said immediately that the concept that all the workings of nature are the moment-by-moment activity of God allows us total freedom to accept such an asymmetry, simply because God possesses the freedom to act as He pleases. However, there is perhaps something of a moral dilemma in this idea of asymmetry between the normal and the miraculous. I have been trying to establish that they are essentially the same thing, namely the expression of God's immediate will, and this asymmetry seems to weaken this idea.

One possible approach to this problem is as follows. Given that God desires to interact with His physical creation in a way that would be manifest to men, the *alternative* to a localized change would be wholly destructive. A *universal* change in the laws of nature, even though it were for a moment of time only, would be destructive of the kind of universe in which we live. Miracles are not a necessary consequence of the existence of God. It is conceivable that God could have remained in that general relationship with creation that is expressed in natural law and described by science. There needed to be no inevitable employment of miracles in God's dealings with the physical world. But had He adopted that approach, it would have been very difficult for man to deduce God's activity from this general 'background' behaviour of the universe. (This is not to ignore the teaching of Romans 1 which shows that man *ought* to deduce God's existence and power from just this evidence, but fails to do so.) The 'exception' of the miraculous draws attention to and 'proves' the rule of God's universal sustenance of nature. So, given that God desires to manifest Himself and demonstrate unmistakably His existence and His interest in the world, how could He rationally go about it? The localized change, giving rise to what we observe as a miracle, seems to me to be the only possible manner in which God could achieve these purposes without a total disruption of the fabric of the universe. Thus the asymmetry we noticed in God's dealings with the physical world is not the stumbling-block that it first appears to be. It is (anthropomorphically speaking) God's only alternative if He wishes to make His presence known physically to men who are blind to the evidence of nature itself concerning His 'power and Godhead'.

Miracle in creation

We have now finished with our definition and must move on to our second topic, namely, miracle in creation. Firstly, all Christians, as far as I am aware, agree that a miracle occurred at the beginning of creation. That is, the *creatio ex nihilo* was a miracle falling within my definition, with the special feature that the 'change' in the laws of nature involved was the actual origination of those laws. It is interesting to note that the concept of an *ex nihilo* creation is peculiarly Judaeo-Christian and although there are many creation myths from different ancient cultures, the idea of a creation from nothing is exclusively biblical in origin. Indeed, even non-Christians are normally forced to admit that the origin of the universe was a miracle in the sense that it can never be explained by science. However, having agreed on that starting-point, Christians, and indeed Bible-believing Christians, then take very different courses. They differ as to the subsequent incidence of the miraculous in the formation of the earth and universe as we know it today. There are those who are theistic evolutionists, not only in the restricted sense of Darwinian evolution, but in the global sense of believing that from the original creation, the whole history of the universe can be described scientifically (non-miraculously) in evolutionary terms. The original 'big bang' was followed by an expansion of the universe which is still observable today by means of the galactic 'red shift'. Clouds of gas cooled and condensed into stars and galaxies. The earth came into being, perhaps as a result of a stellar explosion, and everything that has occurred subsequently upon earth, including the origin and development of life, can be explained by appeal only to the outworking of scientific process. Those who espouse these views are, of course, to some extent inconsistent, at least in so far as they do so to avoid the 'embarrassment' of invoking the miraculous. They allow the miracles of the New Testament; they look forward to a miraculous end to this present age, and yet they rigorously exclude miracle from the process of creation and the formation of our present world.

It is interesting to speculate why some Christians who believe the Bible do adopt this position. I believe that they unwittingly read into the Bible philosophical presuppositions that are themselves extra-biblical. For example, they read in a false view of natural law, namely that these laws are somehow independent of God. They admit that He created them at the beginning, but then somehow left them with an independent existence. As long as one holds this erroneous view, it is quite natural to claim that those laws must have operated inexorably from the beginning of time and that any exception to their operation is inadmissible because it would violate the very rules that God has made. If, however, natural law is understood in the biblical sense, that is, as the immediate expression of the mind of God, then this problem vanishes and the biblical account of creation can be studied without the burden of extra-biblical philosophical constraints.

Thus we come to the question: 'Does the Bible teach that miracles were involved in the formation of the worlds subsequent to the *ex nihilo* creation?' This is not such a straightforward issue as may appear at first sight. I would maintain, however, that the Bible does teach that such miracles occurred, and the three main arguments in favour of this view are as follows. The first is that the events recorded in the first two chapters of Genesis could not possibly have taken place on the time-scale permitted by a straightforward reading of these chapters, if they were caused solely by natural process. There must have been transformations or changes in natural law for these things to have happened in the time allowed by the record. You will immediately recognize at this point the motives of those who seek to introduce long periods of elapsed time into the Genesis narrative, either by allowing that the 'days' were in fact eras of time, or by such artificial devices as the 'gap theory'. And, of course, the 'day-age' theory is followed by many theologically respectable evangelical commentators. But if we read these early chapters of Genesis with a mind innocent of preconceptions, it is inescapable that things were happening at a rate and in a manner that is unknown to science today. It therefore seems to me that there is in these passages of Scripture an unavoidable miraculous element which can only be bypassed by quite extraordinary and unconvincing arguments as to the interpretation of the passages. This matter is considered further in chapter 5.

My second reason for believing that the 'subsequent creation' involved miraculous stages is the repetition in Genesis 1 of the expression: 'And God said . . .'. It seems to me that if the processes described in this chapter were simply natural, the repetition of the phrase, 'And God said', would be quite superfluous. If all that is being described in this chapter are successive steps in a natural evolutionary process, one would expect these words to be littered throughout Scripture on almost every page! The very fact that a fresh pronouncement from God was required for each stage of the creation implies strongly that a non-natural, or miraculous event was about to occur. If this is not the case, I can see no purpose whatsoever for the use, uniquely in this narrative, of the language employed. Admittedly I have argued that the normal course of nature is controlled by God's word, but all that establishes is that the expression 'And God said,' could be applied to miracle and nature alike. My argument is not that the precise words used bear a necessarily miraculous implication, but rather that their unique employment in Genesis 1 and their absence elsewhere in Old Testament writings point to the special character of these events relative to the normality of natural law.

Thirdly, Genesis states plainly that the work of creation was completed on the seventh day. 'Thus the heavens and the earth were finished, and all the host of them. And on the seventh day God ended his work which he had made' (Gen. 2: 1-2). If the creation had been accomplished by the outworkings of natural law it seems inconceivable that such a claim could be made, for natural process continues uninterrupted. The forces which shaped the continents and oceans in Genesis 1 would be the same as those that shape them now. The evolution of the biosphere in the biblical record would be one and the same process as is, allegedly, at work today. There could have been no termination to the work of creation if it were simply the product of natural process. There must have been something distinctive about the six days of creation for them to be represented as a separate era with a distinct end. I suggest that the singularity of that period lay in the performance by God of miraculous creative acts.

What, then, are our alternatives as we regard creation from the point of view of miracles? Firstly, there is the global evolutionary approach, in which the entire universe as we know it today is attributed to the operation of natural process. You may feel that what I have said about the spiritual origin of natural law makes the evolutionary viewpoint *more* acceptable to the Christian rather than less, since it leaves God as the prime mover behind all process even though it be natural rather than miraculous. I must accept that this is indeed the case. While this is philosophically acceptable, however, I am forced to reject 'theistic evolution' purely on biblical grounds, since, as I have just argued, the implication of Scripture is that creation subsequent to the *ex nihilo* beginning involved miraculous acts on the part of God.

Mature creation

The next alternative to 'theistic evolution', the opposite pole of interpretation, is the concept of a 'mature creation', namely that the universe was created largely in the form that we see it today, with the exception that the Noachian flood wrought dramatic changes in the geology and climate of earth. On this view the galaxies and stars, the earth and the moon, the entire biosphere (life in all its forms) and man himself, were created in a period of seven literal days as described in Genesis 1, and have undergone no significant evolutionary change since that time. It does not deny modern cosmological *observation;* it does not imply that there have not been nuclear processes operating in the stars or that such things as supernovae do not occur in remote galaxies. It does not mean that certain changes and adaptations do not take place among living species or that mutations do not occur from time to time. But these are small variations relative to the initial creation. According to 'mature creation' the heavens were created ready-made, together with the light trains which span the immense distances between the stars and earth and by which the former are made visible to us. This implies, of course, that we appear to be seeing cosmic events that took place millions of years ago, but this is a natural consequence of the creation of light *en route,* together with any variations in wavelength and intensity that we may (wrongly) interpret as extremely ancient events.

The mature creation view does give rise to certain problems. It does not provide a glib means of reconciling biblical testimony with modern scientific observation. To begin with, there is a basic philosophical difficulty, namely, that mature creation may be an essentially empty concept. I can put this most dramatically in the following way. You do not know it, and I do not know it, but the universe was, in fact, created at 6 a.m. this morning! The fact that we are all unaware of this is because our memories were created in a mature form along with ourselves. You think that yesterday you did certain things and met certain people. But you are wrong. You think that was the case because your memories came into existence this morning complete with a store of 'recollections' which bear no relation to real events. This is, of course, an argument of *reductio ad absurdum,* yet it represents a valid philosophical objection to the doctrine of mature creation. Of course, as Christians we may argue in reply that the 6 a.m. creation is inadmissible because it would make God a liar, since our Bible, which purports to record real historical events stretching back somewhat earlier than six o'clock this morning, would be totally false. This would be a denial of the character of God and we may therefore dismiss the hypothesis. But we must appreciate that the world of unbelief has no such inhibitions and that they may fairly claim that the concept of mature creation, because it can never be disproved (any more than the six o'clock creation), adds nothing to our understanding and is thus an empty concept.

The second problem with mature creation is that it is *too* exclusive of natural process. It so denigrates 'process' as a participating mechanism in the formation of the universe, that it almost becomes unbiblical in its teaching, suggesting that everything happened in a flash, in a puff of blue smoke as it were, without the lapse of time. In contrast to this, the Bible is quite clear that process *was* involved in creation. It took God six days to bring into being the earth and all that it contains. We cannot eliminate time and process from the creation for the simple reason that the Bible does not eliminate them. A simplistic view of mature creation is thus unbiblical because its suspicion of process leads it to deny the clear teaching of Scripture. We must not allow our reaction against the excesses of evolutionary thinking to drive us to an equally untenable opposite view in which process is treated as a 'dirty word'. Such an overly simplistic approach leads to absurdity as well as a denial of Scripture. It suggests, for example, that matter existed once without coexisting natural law. But you cannot have matter and energy, space and time, without the rules that control their behaviour. Yet in some recent writings it is almost suggested that before the six days of creation had been completed there *was* no scientific law. The whole period was so miraculous as to be beyond discussion or imagination and we cannot allow natural process in any shape or form to intrude into that era. For example, the statement that the earth was 'without form and void' is taken to mean that there was no such thing as gravity at that time, and that the earth was without any kind of shape. I find this unacceptable and there is a real danger that under the banner of mature creation we may go so far out on a limb as to become irrational and illogical, as well as unbiblical.

A middle way

Is there a 'middle way', avoiding these problems and remaining true to the actual record of the Bible? I do not use 'middle' to signify a compromise between evolution and creation, but rather a rational approach which can be justified intellectually as well as remaining true to the belief that Genesis should be read as sober history. In my view, what I have said about the character of scientific law makes it necessary to believe that process (the normal operation of scientific law) and miracle can and did coexist. The existence of one does not exclude the other. We do not have to think of a six-day miraculous creation when no process was permitted, followed by a post-creation era in which all occurrence can be described by science. To dramatize this somewhat, it is perfectly possible and consistent with the biblical account of the creation that fish and the other creatures of the sea were created *de novo* in an aqueous environment obeying all the natural laws of hydrodynamics and hydrostatics, that is, a perfectly normal sea such as we know today. In the midst of that completely natural medium, obeying completely natural laws, a change in the laws of nature occurred by which God brought into being, by miraculous fiat, the hosts of sea-dwelling creatures. It is very obvious, I think, that this must have been the case by comparison with the miracles of the New Testament. To return for a moment to Cana, the wine that was created in the stone jars was produced in vessels which behaved in all respects as natural objects obeying natural law. Everything associated with the miracle, with the sole exception of the water itself, was obeying scientific law at the time the miracle took place. Thus the coexistence within the creation record of miracle and process seems to me to be a necessary deduction from Scripture.

This means, of course, that many of the processes with which biology, geology, physics and chemistry deal, can be associated with the creation, right through from the *ex nihilo* origin of the universe to the completion of the work of creation on the seventh day. It is vital to a proper understanding of Genesis that we allow miraculous fiat to occur as and when stated in the record. But it is perfectly possible that many of the scientific processes that are advanced under the banner of global evolution may also apply and be admissible as processes contributing to the events recorded in the creation narrative. No one is in a position to be dogmatic at this point. We have to be willing, to some extent, to differ on these matters. We have to accept that none of our ideas, in so far as they are not confirmed explicitly by Scripture, can be said to be final and complete. It is quite possible, by way of example, that the original creation *ex nihilo* lay at some time of unspecified duration prior to the dawning of light on earth. In Exodus 20:11 this earlier period would be comprehended in the first day, which, unlike the subsequent days which were delimited by morning and evening, could thus have been of indefinite backward duration. This view would permit the acceptance of a 'big bang' origin of the universe as currently favoured by cosmologists and a 'scientific' model of its evolution. On the other hand, the succession of night and day which delineates the remaining days of creation seems to me to prohibit any scriptural authority for the 'day-age' theory. The other days can only be understood as periods of the rotation of the earth upon its axis.

So then, I believe there is something of a middle way. What we must avoid (and this is the key to the whole matter), is an imposition upon Scripture of foreign philosophical principles, whether the principle involved is called 'evolution' or 'mature creation'. Let Scripture speak.

Providence

Let me move on to the third and final point of my lecture, namely the subject of providence. This is, of course, an enormous subject and I hope you will understand that I am having to deal with it in the limited context of the natural world and our view of science. My treatment is therefore of a somewhat clinical nature. Providence is one of the most glorious doctrines of the Christian faith and of the Bible, and although we shall see something of its anatomy, we shall see little of its true loveliness in this brief consideration.

What do we mean by 'providence'? As we defined the miraculous, so we now need to define providence. My definition is as follows: 'Providence is God's manipulation of natural processes and events to fulfil His purposes.' Thus I draw a clear distinction between miracle and providence in that miracle involves the alteration or change of natural law, whereas providence involves God's *use* of natural law and process to bring about His designs. I also see three different kinds of providence, at least, that we may recognize in Scripture. The first is what I will call *the overall scheme of God's beneficence.* Many Scriptures point to this, for example, Psalm 145:16: 'Thou openest thine hand, and satisfiest the desire of every living thing.' Psalms 65 and 104 are other clear examples: 'Thou visitest the earth, and waterest it: thou greatly enrichest it with the river of God ... thou preparest them corn.' 'He causeth the grass to grow for the cattle, and herb for the service of man.' Admittedly, these statements are highly poetical, but we must beware of thinking that because something is poetical it is somehow less true. These are true and valid statements of fact. The things referred to in the psalms, such as the hydrological cycle of evaporation and rainfall, the cycle of life and death in nature, springtime and harvest, are the consequences of natural law, and thus can properly be described in scientific or naturalistic terms. But since natural law is the word of God's power, since the natural universe is upheld on an instantaneous basis by the will and mind of God, it is also perfectly proper to do what the psalms do, namely to ascribe to the beneficence of God all the functions of natural process and their due results. It is a direct consequence of the doctrine of universal sustenance that these processes may both be *described* by science and *ascribed* to the providence of God. There is no contradiction or 'double-think' involved. So let us not be ashamed of the Bible when, in our scientific age, it speaks of God watering the earth and causing the grass to grow. Let us not dismiss these words as merely poetical and lacking in scientific credibility. In a most profound sense these 'poetical' statements are highly scientific because they take us beyond science to the ground of all being, the spiritual reality, that lies beneath science, namely the being and the mind of God. These biblical claims, far from being subscientific, are valid in a more fundamental sense than any purely scientific statement could ever be.

We come secondly to something I will call *'special providence' in the realm of nature.* We are still thinking about nature but we now consider particular instances of providential care or action on the part of God. An example of this is the crossing of the Red Sea which I deliberately excluded from the realm of the miraculous. This event falls clearly into my definition of special providence. Here we have a sequence of events that, as far as we can tell, took place by natural process but the timing of which was 'miraculous' in the more general sense of that word. These happenings were clearly not just coincidences; they were 'miracles' of timing. Natural events conspired in an extraordinary way to fulfil God's purpose at that moment of history. The provision of quails in the wilderness for the starving Israelites and the earthquake that wrecked the gaol at Philippi provide further instances of natural events which occurred at just the right moment and in just the right manner to give rise to the desired effects in the purposes of God. Jonah's storm is a further case in point. None of these events can be placed in the realm of the miraculous as I have defined that term. They are rather instances of the manipulation of natural, non-miraculous causes by God with a view to achieving certain definite results in the affairs of men and nations.

This brief description of 'special providence' does raise some problems. How, may we ask, does God so direct natural process? In one sense there is more difficulty with this concept than there is with the idea of the miraculous. In the latter we simply say that God 'changed the rules' of nature, so that things took place that could not otherwise have done so. That is quite an easy concept to grasp. But now we are saying that God somehow manipulates the laws of nature without changing them; that He acts to produce specific desired effects within the constraints of natural law. How can this be? How can the rules of nature be manipulated without being altered?

I am not sure that I can provide a complete answer to this particular philosophical difficulty, but I will attempt to point the way to a solution. The first thing to grasp is that natural law, as understood today by scientists, is based upon statistical concepts. In the nineteenth century the climate of opinion among scientists was essentially deterministic. People believed that if it were possible to know the momentum and position of every particle in the universe, it would in principle be possible to predict completely the future course of events, because these would follow as rigorous consequences of the laws of cause and effect. On this view the only bar to a complete prediction of the future was our ignorance of the present! Such determination is, of course, contrary both to our instincts (which lead us to believe that we do possess at least a measure of freedom to determine our own destinies) and to the teaching of Scripture. But it is more germane to my present argument that this nineteenth-century determinism was routed, in the first quarter of our present century, by the introduction into science of quantum mechanical theory. Einstein, as a matter of interest, never did fully accept the idea that all scientific law is ultimately based upon statistical processes. Nevertheless, it is today accepted that scientific law on the macroscopic level (the laws of mechanics, electromagnetics, chemistry and so forth) derive from the statistical outcome of innumerable microscopical (atomic scale) events. To give a simple example, the pressure inside a motor tyre, which appears macroscopically to be a constant measurable quantity, actually arises from the constant bombardment of the inner walls of the tyre by the molecules of gas that it contains, moving in a totally random fashion which can only be described by statistics. So the pressure is not in fact constant. It is subject to continual tiny variations or fluctuations which can indeed be measured with sufficiently sensitive instruments. Once we let go of determinism in science, once we allow that macroscopic laws in nature are the outcome of averaging effects over a vast number of microscopically random events, you will recognize that there is room for indeterminism; for a variable outcome. And there is therefore room in natural science for the involvement of God in determining the precise outcome in nature of the operation of natural law. There is room for the manipulation of the infinitely complex interactions of laws to produce, for example, an earthquake in one place rather than another, at a set time rather than a different one, and of an intensity calculated to achieve a particular effect. I do not pretend to have answered completely this profound problem of how the providence of God works on a physical and natural plane, but I hope these thoughts may point the way to its solution.

The third type of providence I want to mention can be described as *God's providence mediated through human behaviour.* The first two classes of providential action are, as we have seen, concerned with the physical world, not necessarily involving human participation. But there is clearly a third kind of providence that is mediated through human behaviour. There are many examples in Scripture. God hardened Pharaoh's heart, and this gave rise to certain important consequences in the histories of both Egypt and Israel. God stirred up the spirit of Cyrus, king of Persia, so that he was instrumental in the restoration of Jerusalem under Zerubbabel. Nebuchadnezzar was taught that the 'Most High ruleth in the kingdoms of men' and He does so by manipulating the minds and hearts of men. This kind of providence presents no difficulty at all, because as we saw previously, God is spirit and mind and it is therefore a logical consequence that God has total freedom and capacity to act upon the minds of men to sway and to direct them, so that they become His agents whether willingly or not. Clearly this applies not only to men like Pharaoh and Cyrus, but even more so to the believer who is concerned from the outset to discover and obey the will of God. I shall not dwell upon this aspect of providence further since it seems to present no difficulty to the rational mind and fits in very simply to the theological and scientific worldview that I have tried to present in these lectures.

Human accountability

So we come finally and briefly to the subject of human accountability to God. Let me repeat what I said earlier, that my treatment of the subject of providence in this lecture has of necessity been a somewhat clinical one and one in which the true glory of God in providence has been implicit rather than explicit. But in this final section, as we approach the subject of accountability, we do begin to close with the more human and personal aspects of our theme.

I hope that in the course of these lectures, whatever else we have or have not seen, we have grasped something of the immediacy of God. This is the thread which has run throughout my remarks, whether concerning the *ex nihilo* creation, the miraculous or providence. God is here. God is present and at work in all things at all times. 'In all life Thou livest, the true life of all.' And this concept of the immediacy of God has the capacity to transform all I have said from dry theology and philosophy into the warmth and reality of an awareness of God. The immediacy of God is the lodestone that can infuse all our meditation with the immanent glory of the

living God. The whole burden of what I have said leads to the
conclusion of the apostle Paul, namely that God 'is not far
from every one of us, for in Him we live, and move, and have
our being'. We have seen the immediacy of God in the doctrine of universal sustenance, in our concept of the miraculous, in general providence, in special providence and in providence mediated through human behaviour. And even as we
contemplate these things from a philosophical and scientific
viewpoint, God closes in upon us. He does so to such a degree
that we may well begin to tremble, even by virtue of the un-
varnished philosophical ideas that have concerned us in this
lecture. Jesus Christ said of God the Father: 'Fear him who
is able to destroy . . .' If I may be allowed to truncate that
Scripture, we may say, 'Fear Him who is able', who has power
and authority, who holds the breath of every living creature
in His hand. Fear Him whose presence and will alone uphold
the very existence of the physical universe in which we live.
Fear that invisible Reality that lies behind and within the
visible world. Let us order our priorities aright and, with the
apostle, 'look not at the things which are seen, but at the
things which are not seen; for the things which are seen are
temporal, but the things which are not seen are eternal'.
These unseen things represent the ultimate spiritual reality
that we call God and, by the grace of Jesus Christ, Father.

The immediacy of God, it seems to me, lays upon all
men the responsibility to seek to know Him. Paul declares,
'God . . . hath made of one blood all nations of men . . . and
hath determined the times . . . and the bounds of their habi-
tation; *that they should seek the Lord* . . . and find him,
though he be not far from every one of us' (Acts 17:26-28).
Our life is so grounded in the life of God that to neglect to
seek Him is a denial of our own human nature. If we do
neglect it we shall surely be called to account, for it is the
duty of the creature to know and recognize his Creator. The
concept of duty is, of course, a moral one and stems from
the fact that God and man alike have a moral element in
their natures. Yet human moral responsibility is only another
manifestation of the unity God imposes upon the universe, a
unity we have examined in the context of science. *We* are
morally responsible to God because we are made in the image
of a moral Deity.

CHAPTER FIVE

In this chapter we return to the debate introduced in chapter 2, namely the conflict between evolution and creation. Here the question under scrutiny is the admissibility of theistic evolution as a means of synthesizing the theory of evolution with the biblical testimony regarding creation and human origins. The essay devotes most of its attention to the conflict between evolutionary and scriptural world-views, but also contains a positive restatement of the biblical theory of being that has already been considered in chapters 3 and 4.

The biblical and philosophical case for special creation

Introduction

Although much has been written on the scientific aspects of the creation versus evolution debate, relatively few recent authors have considered the matter at the philosophical level. Yet there are two very good reasons for so doing. Firstly, it is only at this level that common conceptual ground exists for the scientific and biblical viewpoints. The Bible makes no direct contribution to a discussion, say, of genetic mutations or electromagnetic theory, neither has science anything to say about the origin of matter or the doctrine of the Holy Spirit. There is no self-evident meeting-point between the two at the basic levels of pragmatic science and spiritual truth. Indeed this realization has led to the idea that there exists a 'complementarity' between the scientific and religious world-views in which both represent more or less complete and self-contained descriptions of reality. There is, however, a deeper level at which common conceptual ground does exist, and it is the weakness of 'complementarity' that it fails adequately to explore this ground. This is the level at which we ask, 'What is the nature of science and scientific theory? Whence are the laws of science? Why are they as they are, and not otherwise? How far does scientific theory describe reality? What are the ultimate limitations of science?' It is also the level at which we discuss the theological concepts of creation *ex nihilo*, miracles and providence, as well as the extent of the authority and inspiration of Scripture. These are philosophical questions and *only on this plane* is it ultimately relevant to compare and contrast the testimonies of science and the Bible.

Secondly, as I hope to demonstrate, the conflict between

the concepts of creation and evolution is in the final analysis not a case of science versus religion but of one philosophy against another. It is a self-evident fact, which is none the less frequently ignored, that no scientific theory or experiment can prove that chemical evolution or neo-Darwinian transformation have actually occurred historically. They can at best provide a rational basis for the *belief* that these processes occurred. Science can 'prove' to everyone's satisfaction that a historical event such as the formation of a limestone cave occurred by the action of water acidified by atmospheric carbon dioxide. (Though even here one must add the proviso that the laws of chemistry as we know them today were in operation at the time.) What is quite impossible to 'prove' in this same sense is that unique past events such as the origin of life, which cannot be reproduced in the laboratory and represent vast extrapolations of current scientific experience, did actually occur by natural process. A belief in evolution, therefore, is just that – a belief. It is a belief rationalized by appeal to scientific observation, just as Christian belief is rationalized on the basis of a different kind of current human experience. I submit therefore that the creationist and evolutionist are alike in exercising faith in (different) interpretations of nature which are not susceptible of scientific proof.

In order to address ourselves to these matters at the biblical and philosophical levels we need to consider a number of related matters. These will by no means exhaust the subject and in some areas may not lead us to clear-cut answers. They will, however, serve to introduce us to a level of debate which may clarify many of the issues and demonstrate the creationist position on origins to be both rational and scientific in the deepest sense of that word.

In what follows, we are going to look first at the conflicts which exist, to the writer's mind, between the biblical and evolutionary accounts of origins, both biological and abiogenic. These conflicts do not, as some imagine, reside exclusively in an unduly literal interpretation of Genesis 1 and 2, but involve the total world-view of Scripture in both Old and New Testaments. It is for this reason that I use the word 'philosophical' to describe the level of debate involved in this conflict.

Our second task will be to examine the theory of evolution
to establish how far it can properly be described as a scientific
theory at all. Once again we shall find ourselves treading
ground which is philosophical rather than scientific in character. We shall look in turn at the three aspects of the evolutionary view, namely chemical evolution (the origin of life),
neo-Darwinian evolution (organic evolution) and the fossil
record. Finally we present a synthesis of biblical and scientific
ideas that I have previously termed a 'theology of science'[1]
and which provides a unified treatment of scientific law,
miracles, creation and providence. Naturally enough, each of
these subjects will have to be dealt with concisely and the
reader is referred elsewhere for a fuller treatment.[2,3]

Conflicts between evolution and the Bible

There are both Christian creationists and evolutionists who,
equally, accept that the Bible as originally written is a
unique, inspired revelation from God to man, mediated
through human authors who were not only guided positively
in their writing, but also protected from error. We reject the
compromise view of inspiration which has recently gained
some currency, that the Scriptures are infallible as regards
spiritual truth but contain errors of fact and history arising
from the scientific and historical ignorance of the writers.[4,5]
We also reject the view that much of the Old Testament is
mythological, both in the normal sense of that word and in
the theological sense of myth as a non-historical vehicle for
spiritual truth. It is a unique feature of the Christian religion
that its spiritual teaching is inextricably bound up with
human history and stands or falls by the accuracy of its
historical record. The most obvious example is the death
and resurrection of Jesus Christ, the historicity of which
events form the basis of the Christian gospel. But the
historical reality of creation is equally basic to the character of God as revealed in Scripture (see for example, Psalm
33:6; 90:2; 104:24; 148:2-5; Isaiah 40:25-29; Amos 4:13;
Romans 1:25). If creation is, historically speaking, a myth,
then the credentials of the God of the Bible are irretrievably
destroyed.

The questions that remain, therefore, are:

a. Whether the accounts of and references to creation recorded in Genesis and other parts of Scripture are *intended* to be read as sober history; or whether, instead, they are allegorical and poetical without claiming to give factual details;

b. Whether the biblical teaching on creation, providence, the Fall and the flood can be reconciled with evolutionary concepts. The answer to this may, of course, depend greatly on our answer to *a.*

Let us examine these questions.

The historicity of Genesis

It is a basic principle of biblical interpretation that the nature of any piece of writing it contains can be ascertained. Thus poetry, allegory, parable and history must each be recognizable as such either by virtue of its internal structure, its context or on the evidence of other portions of Scripture. On each of these tests, the early chapters of Genesis emerge as unmistakably historical in intent.

The major passages involved are, of course, Genesis 1 to 3, which contain the accounts of creation and the Fall, and chapters 6 to 9 covering the story of Noah and the flood. The internal structure of these passages is that of a straightforward narrative, with no evidence of typical Hebrew poetical forms[6] and no 'commentary' to suggest that the events described should not be taken factually (as, for example, in Numbers 23:7 *et seq.* and Job 27:1). It has been suggested that the thematic repetition in Genesis 1 ('and the evening and the morning . . .') is indicative of poetical content. But repetition of a theme is common in Hebrew narrative, other examples being: 'These are the generations . . .' (Genesis 2:4; 5:1; 6:9; 11:10; 11:27 etc.); 'All the people shall . . . say, Amen' (Deuteronomy 27:15-26); 'Blessed (cursed) shalt thou be' (Deuteronomy 28:3,4,5,6,16,17,18,19). Thematic repetition is therefore a device of Hebrew literature indeed, but carries no implications of an allegorical treatment of the subject matter.

Another proposal,[7] developed by Noordtzij,[8] Ridderbos[9] and Kline,[10] and known as the 'framework hypothesis', suggests that Genesis 1 is not chronological but parallel. Thus days one and four deal with 'the realm of light', days two and five with the realm of 'water' and days three and six with the realm of 'land'. Thus, it is proposed, Genesis 1 is a topical rather than chronological account of creation, with the further implication of a 'less historical' and more allegorical character. But such a parallelism surely exists more in the minds of the interpreters than in the text. For one thing, any symmetry which might exist in the passage is broken by the seventh day, while the deliberate numbering of the days is surely intended to convey *sequence* if nothing else! A full refutation of the framework hypothesis has been offered by E.J. Young.[11]

A further argument against a poetical or allegorical reading of Genesis 1 lies in the fact that the Scriptures contain *elsewhere* such poetical descriptions of creation. Psalm 104:1-23 is clearly based on the Genesis account of creation. It is not only cast in a poetical form, but employs the universal devices of poetic writing such as metaphor (vv. 1-5), simile (v. 6), anthropomorphism (vv. 13,19) and so on. We do not really suppose the psalmist to think that God uses clouds as literal chariots or occupies some stratospherical chamber from which He decants water upon the earth. This is evident poetry. Another such passage is Job 38, where creation is described by such metaphors as a builder laying the foundations of a house, a stellar oratorio, and birth from the womb. All this is obvious and very beautiful poetry, wholly distinct from the unembroidered 'action' language of Genesis 1. Quite apart from the self-evident literary contrast is the consideration that poets frequently celebrate historical events in their verse, but seldom write poems about other poems! The psalms in particular dwell upon the historical records of Israel or the historical (that is, real life) experience of the writers. By analogy one would expect the creation poems of Psalms and Job to be based upon factual recorded history rather than pre-existent allegory.

Let us look, secondly, at the context of the passages in question. We have already argued that the internal structure of Genesis 1-3 and 6-9 provides no support for a non-historical interpretation, and we now turn to the second criterion of historicity. The accounts of both creation and flood are set in the uncompromisingly historical context of the entire book of Genesis. No one, I think, denies the historicity of Abraham and the patriarchs, nor is the historical intent of chapters 4-5 in question, containing as they do the pre-Noachian genealogy. This genealogy is incorporated into the lineage of Christ in Luke 3 and is unquestionably regarded as historical by that careful chronicler. Not only is this historical section, Genesis 4-5, sandwiched between the creation story and the flood narrative, but the whole of Genesis is bound together as a unity by the periodic repetition of the expression: 'These are the generations of . . .' or similar words. This refrain occurs in 2:4; 5:1; 6:9; 10:1; 11:10; 25:12; 36:1; 37:2 and joins the creation and flood narratives, indissolubly, to the acknowledged historical sections of Genesis. Only chapter 1 might (on some views) be held to lie outside the historical framework established by this formula, but it would seem quite illogical for the writer of Genesis to have attached an allegorical preface to what is otherwise a uniformly historical narrative. We therefore maintain that the creation and flood epics are, from their context, wholly historical in intent.

Finally we apply the third criterion of historicity, namely the testimony of other Scriptures. Firstly, the argument from silence is not without force. Nowhere in Old or New Testaments is there the slightest suggestion that Adam, Noah, the creation or the flood are figurative or mythological. For example, the apostle John provides himself with an excellent opportunity for reinterpreting the creation story when, in the prologue to his Gospel, he identifies Christ as the 'Logos', the agent of God's creative activity. Yet he not only implies a literal creation but actually borrows his phraseology from Genesis 1:1. Again, the apostle Paul employs the physically creative action of Genesis 1 to illustrate the spiritually creative work of salvation: 'God, who commanded the light to shine out of darkness, hath shined in our hearts, to give the light of the knowledge of the glory of God in the face of Jesus Christ' (2 Corinthians 4:6). The clear implication is that Paul accepted Genesis 1:3 as a historical event, for otherwise it loses all force as an illustration of the spiritual fiat of regeneration.

Peter adds his testimony in 2 Peter 3:3-8. Not only does he refer to the creation story ('By the word of God the heavens were of old, and the earth standing out of the water') but also to the deluge ('The world that then was, being overflowed with water, perished'). Nor is this an isolated statement, for the same writer elsewhere (1 Peter 3:20) uses Noah and his salvation in the ark to illustrate both God's judgement and deliverance in the spiritual realm.

The historicity of Adam and Eve, and of the Fall, is attested by Paul in Romans 5:12-21. It is not sufficient to dismiss this passage by saying, as some do, that Paul was simply using the 'Adamic myth' to bring home a spiritual lesson. The historical reality of the disobedience of one man is essential to the argument being presented here. Indeed it is also essential to insist that the one man in question was the unique ancestor of the human race, for otherwise 'death' could not have 'passed upon all men' and the doctrine of original sin would be negated. If Christ and Moses ('Death reigned from Adam to Moses') are characters of history, the conclusion is inescapable that Adam was also. If Christ's act of atonement is an event embedded in the matrix of human history, so also was Adam's act of rebellion. The apostle, at least, seems under no illusions at this point.

We see, then, that by the tests of internal structure, context and biblical testimony, the Genesis accounts of creation and the flood must be taken as entirely historical in intent. Those theistic evolutionists who teach otherwise do so on criteria that are wholly extra-biblical, as D.A. Young has argued convincingly.[12] The criteria in question are, for example, the presupposition that the Bible is accurate only on matters of spiritual truth and not of science or history. More fundamentally, perhaps, such commentators, though sometimes evangelical in name, implicitly elevate the ultimate authority of human reason above the final authority of Scripture. Thus they feel quite *free* to adopt criteria of biblical interpretation which are extraneous (and antagonistic) to the rules provided by Scripture itself. A prime example of this kind of treatment is the idea, forcefully expounded by Bernard Ramm,[13] that the Genesis flood was a local phenomenon, in spite of categorical assertions both in Genesis 6-9 and 2 Peter 3 of its universality! The argument adopted is that the geological record (as interpreted by uniformitarian science) contains no evidence of a universal inundation and that the biblical testimony must be reinterpreted accordingly. Such attempts lead to a total contradiction of the actual statements of the Scripture and thus, at the very best, an abandonment of the rule of the perspicuity of Scripture.

In short, any attempt to deny the historicity of the early chapters of Genesis leads to quite insoluble problems of biblical interpretation throughout Old and New Testaments. For the liberal theologian, of course, this does not matter for he has no time for the doctrine of verbal inspiration. For the theologically conservative, however, the concession (often unconscious) that modern scientific theories must take precedence over the plain meaning of Scripture is the beginning of a slippery slope indeed. It is not sufficient, as some seem to think, to say that the Bible is not a scientific textbook and should not therefore be accorded authority in the interpretation of nature. If Genesis is *history,* then regardless of the particular paradigm employed to record the historical events, the biblical testimony on creation and historical geology *must* be taken into account (and, indeed, conceded the primary place) in the construction of our cosmogenetical world-view.

Can we reconcile the biblical and evolutionary viewpoints?

Having concluded that the creation and flood narratives of Genesis must be read as history, we now address the second question posed earlier. Is it possible to reconcile the biblical accounts with the modern evolutionary world-view? Many Christians who accept that Genesis *is* history claim that such a reconciliation is possible.

Before we approach the question of reconciliation, we must obviously set out the areas of apparent conflict. These are concisely stated as follows.

a. The age of the earth, and the time-scale of the fossil record, are reckoned in terms of thousands of millions of years by evolution and uniformitarian geology. This is in contrast to the seven-day creation cycle and the genealogical records of Genesis, which seem to place the creation of Adam no more than about ten thousand years ago, even admitting that the genealogies are incomplete.

b. According to conventional thinking, the process of evolution is ongoing, operating now as it has always operated in the past. In contrast, the creation recorded in Genesis was complete and finished at some past juncture ('On the seventh day God ended his work which he had made' – Genesis 2:2).

c. Evolution envisages a continuous improvement of the biosphere, as more complex and adapted forms of life arise with the passage of time. Though temporary setbacks are not ruled out, evolution has a general 'upward' tendency away from imperfection (poor adaptation) towards perfection (total adaptation). In contrast, the creation recorded in Genesis was originally perfect ('God saw every thing that he had made and, behold, it was very good' – Genesis 1:31). However, as a consequence of Adam's Fall, the whole of nature has undergone degeneration ('Cursed is the ground for thy sake . . . thorns also and thistles shall it bring forth to thee' – Genesis 3:17,18; 'The whole creation groaneth and travaileth in pain together until now' – Romans 8:22), but will one day be restored ('The creation itself also will be set free from its slavery to corruption . . .' – Romans 8:21, NASV). In particular, the Fall is an essential ingredient in the Bible's presentation of salvation through Christ.

d. Theistic evolution allows only a single creation miracle, namely the creation *ex nihilo* of matter and energy. The Genesis account appears to involve a succession of miraculous creative acts, each prefaced by the words: 'And God said, let . . .'

e. As a corollary of *d,* evolution appeals only to natural law and process as an explanation of the appearance of life, its diversification and the rise of man, while the Bible suggests that divine fiat was necessary not only for creation *ex nihilo* but also for the creation of life from non-life, the creation of separate life forms and the origin of man.

f. A miraculous creation and Fall explain the moral problem of sin and suffering. The theistic evolutionary world-view requires that chance, suffering and cruelty (for example, the survival of the fittest) are intrinisic parts of God's creative activity, thus posing insoluble moral questions.

There may well be points of difference between the creationist and evolutionary world-views which do not appear in the above list, or which could have been made more explicit, but these six issues certainly comprehend the major conflicts which confront us as we approach the problem of reconciling current 'scientific' theories of origins with the testimony of Scripture. Before dealing with these conflicts in greater detail I would like to make a general point, namely, that so much effort has been devoted to the question of the age of the earth, both by creationists and theistic evolutionists, that the other five areas of conflict enumerated above have been largely ignored. Yet, in the writer's view, these more theological and philosophical questions are by far the most important ones! Even if one of the simpler methods of reconciling the time-scales of evolution and Genesis, such as the day-age theory, were universally accepted, the five areas of conflict denoted *b* to *f* would remain acute. Until theistic evolution can offer solutions to *these* problems, the evolutionary world-view must remain antagonistic to the general teaching of the Bible.

The age of the earth

In this section we are not concerned to question the conventional geological time-scale but only to see how far the biblical record can be reconciled with it. We shall look more closely at the scientific validity of 'geological time' in a subsequent discussion. Since whole books have been written on this subject, we can here only outline the attempts that have been made to reconcile a six-day creation with the thousands of millions of years demanded by current geological and evolutionary thinking.

Firstly, and most simply, the 'days' of Genesis 1 may be taken as long periods of time (the 'day-age' theory). This viewpoint has been set out succinctly by Buswell[14] and recently reviewed and advocated by D.A. Young[15] who, as a geologist, is committed equally to the historicity of Genesis and to the geological time-scale. It has been reviewed and rejected by Fields.[16] The main argument in support of the day-age theory is that the seventh day, on which God rested from His creative work, is still in progress and thus must represent an epoch rather than a literal twenty-four hour day. If this is so, of course, there is no need to insist that the first six days are literal days either. Against this interpretation it may be argued that the expression 'God rested' can be taken to mean 'God ceased', or 'God began to rest' referring to an instantaneous event which could indeed have occurred on a literal seventh day. The implied translation of 'God rested' as 'God rested throughout the seventh day' is required neither by the text nor by the Jewish sabbath which celebrates the completion of creation. Indeed the full statement is: 'On the seventh day God ended his work which he had made; and he rested on the seventh day from all his work . . .' (Genesis 2:2). This seems to imply that both the 'ending' and the 'resting' were completed, instantaneous actions without any extension in time. The verb 'to end' *must* carry this instantaneous significance and 'to rest' *may* also do so. If this is the case, the seventh day could clearly be a literal day, and the chief support for the day-age theory collapses.

It is often assumed that God's resting on the seventh day must imply duration because the Jewish sabbath, based on the creation account, specifies a *duration* (a whole day) for man's resting from *his* labours. A moment's thought, however, shows that it is impossible to draw too close a parallel between the creation week and man's working week simply because, unlike God, man must resume his labours once the sabbath is past. It is quite consistent therefore to suggest that God ceased or began to rest on a literal seventh day (and continued to rest from creative acts on the eighth day and for ever thereafter) and that this fact is permanently commemorated by a seven-day cycle in human society.

Creationists also argue that the Hebrew word *yom* always signifies a literal day unless the context demands otherwise[17] and that references to 'evening and morning' point clearly to an alternation of day and night such as normal days would require. The division of light from darkness (Genesis 1:4) would also be most naturally construed in terms of the earth being illuminated from one direction so that half the globe was in darkness and half in light. This again implies that a day was the period of rotation of earth on its axis. In summary, therefore, the internal evidence for the day-age theory is tenuous in the extreme and the 'normal day' interpretation is most consistent with the usage of *yom* and with the various details of the narrative. Having said this, no one can claim that the matter is proven either way. The writer *could* have intended a figurative use of *yom,* although there really is no convincing internal evidence in favour of the idea. Furthermore, the day-age theory leads to an unnatural interpretation of the succession of light and darkness and their mutual separation as described in Genesis 1. (That is, they too must become figurative, and where does one stop?)

One way to avoid these difficulties is to speculate that the rate of rotation of the earth was originally much slower than at present so that a literal day was much longer than twenty-four hours. Thus today the moon experiences a 'day' of infinite length with respect to the earth as a source of light, while other planets have solar days many hundreds of times longer than earth. This reconciliation of literal days with epochs clearly requires an explanation of how the earth came to possess its present angular momentum. A further speculation is that time itself may have changed in some manner since the creation week, a concept less obnoxious to the scientific mind since Einstein's general theory of relativity was propounded. Most evolutionists would not find this idea appealing, however, because it undermines their concept of unchanging physical law (the basic dogma of evolution) just as drastically as does the six-times-twenty-four-hour creation week. I emphasize that these attempts at reconciliation are speculative and not at present susceptible to proof or disproof.

The second major attempt to reconcile the biblical and geological time-scales resides in the 'gap theory' which proposes that the geological ages are encompassed between verses 1 and 2 of Genesis 1. Verse 2 is then read to mean: 'And the earth *became* without form and void,' signifying a judgement and destruction of a formerly created and populated earth. The fossil record, it is claimed, dates from this stupendous judgement. The 'creation' described in the remainder of Genesis 1 then becomes a recent re-creation in seven literal days. The 'gap theory', popularized by footnotes in the Schofield Bible, has been reviewed and refuted at length in a recent book by W.W. Fields[16] and the reader is referred to that work for further detail. In brief, however, the gap theory is based upon an inadmissible grammatical and philological treatment of the Hebrew text of Genesis 1:1-2 and receives little support from the remainder of Scripture.

One verse often quoted in its favour is Isaiah 45:18: 'For thus saith the Lord that created the heavens; God himself that formed the earth and made it; he hath established it, he created it not in vain [lit. a waste], he formed it to be inhabited.' Thus it is argued that the earth was not created in the state described in Genesis 1:2 but must have become waste at some subsequent time. However, this is surely a misunderstanding of both Isaiah and Genesis. The final clause of Isaiah's verse makes it clear that he is speaking of God's *intention.* He did not create the earth with the *purpose* of its being waste but with the *purpose* that it would become inhabited. Genesis describes the earth as 'formless and void' only at an intermediate state in its development towards a completed, inhabitable condition, not in its final form. There is not the slightest conflict, therefore, between Isaiah and the traditional interpretation of Genesis 1:2.

As indicated earlier, the precise arguments for and against the gap theory turn on linguistic details in the Hebrew text and are too detailed to rehearse here. The present writer, however, would follow Fields in concluding that the theory is no more than a speculation born of the desire to fit geological time into a historical Genesis framework.

A variant of the gap theory is that a 'gap' or time expanse is implied *before* verse 1 of Genesis 1. To establish this idea it is necessary to read verse 1 as a conditional clause qualifying verse 2 (or perhaps verse 3): 'In the beginning of God's creating the heaven and the earth . . . the earth was without form and void.' The effect of this is (a) to produce an involved sentence quite at variance with the crisp style in which the remainder of the chapter is written, and (b) to expunge from Genesis 1 any reference to creation *ex nihilo,* a doctrine clearly taught elsewhere in Scripture (Hebrews 11:3). For these reasons this theory has not attracted widespread support.

Fields is careful to distinguish between the gap theory, which involves the destruction and re-creation of life on earth, and the idea that an indeterminate period of time elapsed between the original creation of 'the heaven and the earth' (v. 1) and the creation of light on earth (v. 3). It can be argued that an indefinite period is admissible during which the earth existed but was 'without form' (featureless?) and 'void' (empty of life?). The only difficulty with this view is the statement in Exodus 20:11: 'In six days the Lord made heaven and earth, the sea, and all that in them is . . .' It is possible to suggest, however, that the first day can be extended backwards indefinitely to include the period of darkness preceding the advent of light (v. 3), if only because there would be no other straightforward way of comprehending this period in a statement such as Exodus 20:11. (Notice that this extension of day one cannot, like the extension of day seven discussed previously, be used to imply that the other days were also long periods of time since, unlike the first day, *they* were bounded by mornings and evenings.)

This 'extended period' interpretation of Genesis 1:2 can provide a partial reconciliation with geological time in that it affords time for the earth to be formed from interstellar material by natural process and could also account for the radiometric ages of igneous and non-fossiliferous metamorphic and sedimentary rocks. It does not, however, permit the great ages attributed to the fossil record nor sufficient time for the natural evolution of life and the biosphere.

The third method of reconciliation will be only mentioned here in passing, namely that Genesis 1 merely describes the revelation to Adam, over a seven-day period, of the facts of creation.[18] According to this view, the six days do not refer to the time-period of creation at all, but only to the period of revelation. This engaging idea seems, however, to contradict flatly Exodus 20:11 ('In six days the Lord *made* . . .'), and also the plain meaning of such words as, 'On the seventh day God ended his work.' It is surely inadmissible to rewrite this verse: 'On the seventh day God ended the revelation of His work,' and yet such rewriting is necessitated by the theory in question.

To summarize, therefore, the various attempts to reconcile fully the geological time-scale with a historical interpretation of Genesis 1 all fail to rise above the level of speculation and also introduce interpretative problems at least as great as those they solve. Under these circumstances, and in the absence of further light on the matter, it would seem wise to accept that Genesis teaches a straightforward miraculous creation of earth and its biosphere in six days, each day being the earth's period of rotation on its own axis. It seems to the writer that the first day only may legitimately be extended backwards in time to encompass the original (and equally miraculous) creation of the universe and the 'formless' earth at some indefinitely prior time, though many creationists would argue that even this possibility is excluded by Exodus 20:11.

Is creation finished?

We have devoted considerable space to the first area of conflict between evolution and the Bible simply because the time-scale issue is the one to which most attention has been directed. It will be possible to deal with the remaining five areas much more concisely, not because they are less important, but simply because theistic evolution seems to offer very little to support its position in respect of these matters.

The completed nature of biblical creation is evident both from Genesis 2:1-2 ('God ended his work . . . and he rested on the seventh day from all his work which he had made') and from the past tense employed in John 1:3 and other Scriptures. At the same time the Bible maintains that God is ever active in *providence,* 'upholding all things by the word of his power' (Hebrews 1:3). Thus a clear distinction is drawn between a past, completed creation and a present, on-going providence. Theistic evolution, however, maintains that God's creative work was executed by means of the ongoing evolutionary process which is still operative today. Thus creation is not yet complete, and providence cannot be clearly distinguished from creation. It seems extremely difficult to reconcile these concepts with the Bible's insistence that creation was fully completed at some past era.

Two possible arguments are available to theistic evolution. The first is that evolution may be assymptotic, that is, rapid at first but tending to a stationary condition so that the major part of all potential evolution has already occurred. In this sense creative evolution might be said to have exhausted its potential and be 'finished'. A second argument is similar but somewhat different, namely that evolution achieved its highest potential in the emergence of man and in that sense only can be held to have 'ended'. All subsequent (and thus current) evolution leads to elaboration and diversification of the biosphere without promoting it to any higher plane.

These arguments face two major difficulties. Firstly, of course, they side-step the plain implication of Scripture which says that God 'rested . . . from *all* his work'. This seems to be such a categorical statement of a fully finished creation as to leave no room for any kind of major subsequent diversification of life forms. The second problem is that these arguments contradict the basic tenet of evolutionary theory, namely that all past biological development occurred by natural processes observable today. If this were true, there is clearly no ground for saying that the future course of evolution will differ in any significant way from its past. If great changes have taken place in the past through the agencies of mutation and natural selection, then there is no reason why they should not continue to do so. In particular there is no basis for the idea that evolution has exhausted its potential or that it has, in man, yet spawned its 'highest possible achievement'. In reality, therefore, the arguments appeal to evolution *plus* its regulation by God in such a way that events occurred in the past which are prohibited today by divine intervention. But this undermines the fundamental uniformitarian concept that past evolution can be wholly explained by processes observable today. The Bible teaching of a finished creation seems to present insuperable difficulties, therefore, to a consistent doctrine of theistic evolution.

Evolution or degeneration?

As indicated earlier, evolution teaches a progressive 'upward' tendency while Scripture relates the story of a perfect creation which has undergone degeneration. How may this 'directional conflict' be resolved? Clearly, theistic evolution can subscribe to a moral and spiritual degeneracy on the part of mankind as a whole. What it cannot embrace, however, is a literal 'Fall' of the first man Adam, since there was no such single man but only an evolving population which emerged from apehood into manhood. Neither can evolutionary thinking accept the idea that the Fall of man led to a degeneracy in the natural order, as taught in Genesis 3 and Romans 8. It is very difficult to spiritualize away the contrast between the initial creation, which was 'very good', and the present natural order, 'subject to vanity' and in 'the bondage of corruption' described in Romans 8. Once again, therefore, a reconciliation between biblical doctrine and theistic evolution seems impossible.

It should perhaps be made clear at this point that the creationist view does not necessarily require that death was unknown in the animal and vegetable kingdoms before the Fall, nor that the laws of physics underwent change at that time. For example, some suggest that the second law of thermodynamics did not operate before the Fall.[19] Clearly *some* forms of death and decay were intrinsic to the original creation of the 'tree yielding fruit, whose seed was in itself' (Genesis 1:12) since flower and fruit both decay before seed is released. Again such phenomena as friction (without which we could neither walk nor grip), and the elasticity of, for example, skin, derive from the second law of thermodynamics! It is not necessary to make extravagant claims to fortify the biblical teaching that some fundamental change took place in the natural order, introducing suffering, disease and human death, and rendering nature subject to 'the bondage of corruption'. The point to grasp at this juncture, however, is that theistic evolution finds it very difficult to make room in its uniformitarian scheme for the physical consequences of the spiritual Fall of Adam, nor indeed for the deliverance and restoration of the natural order so clearly promised in the New Testament.

Creation, miraculous or natural?

Evolution can allow a single creative act, namely the origination from nothing of matter and energy. Intrinsic in this initial act are the creation also of space, time and natural law. From that moment onwards, however, the physical universe is supposed to have developed and evolved by the operation of physical law without the further intervention of divine fiat or creative activity. The creationist justifiably asks why further miraculous acts should be ruled out in respect of origins when theistic evolutionists allow that 'modern' miracles, such as the resurrection of Jesus Christ, have indeed taken place. Theistic evolution seems to be guided by philosophical principles which are wholly extra-biblical in so rigorously excluding any miraculous actions subsequent to the creation of energy and matter. The miraculous creation of life, for example, from existing inanimate chemicals ('dust') would seem a minor problem when set against the *ex nihilo* creation of matter itself.

The Genesis account of creation is most naturally interpreted as a succession of miraculous acts, each introduced by the words: 'And God said, Let . . .' Of course, it is possible to maintain that this repeated expression simply records the various progressive stages of geological and biological evolution as they occurred. But if nothing is intended by these words other than a providential guiding of natural process, it is difficult to see why they are uniquely employed in the creation account and not on every other page of Scripture! The clear implication of such phrases as, 'Let there be . . . and there was', is that some event took place by the direct intent of God which *would not otherwise have happened,* (that is, would not have occurred by natural process). If this were not the case it is difficult to see why such language is used at all.

It might be argued that miracle is necessarily invoked for creation *ex nihilo,* because science offers no explanation for such an event, but that where there exists a scientific theory, miraculous explanations become redundant. Let it be clearly understood, however, that existing scientific knowledge *has* no explanation for the origin of life or for the diversification of the biological kingdom. The evolutionary theories of biogenesis and biological transformism lie in the realm of speculation, not established scientific theory.[2] But even were it possible to offer a genuinely scientific theory of evolution, this would not in any way invalidate a biblical claim that the relevant events did, in fact, occur miraculously. There are some Bible miracles which could not have been achieved by any natural process known to man (for example, the origin of the universe), but others actually employed natural means (the parting of the Red Sea by means of a wind was a miracle of timing, not of means) and yet others might some day be capable of imitation by man (the raising of the recently dead, perhaps?). The primary issue is not therefore whether a given event *could* have occurred by natural process but whether it *did*. The language of Genesis together with the uniform testimony of Scripture to the distinction between miracle and nature point to a multi-stage creation by miraculous *fiat*.

A compromise position known as 'progressive creation'[20] has been proposed, which accepts that Genesis describes a succession of miraculous acts such as the creation of life and of the major types of living organism. These creative acts, however, are widely separated in time (day-age theory) and interspersed by periods of normal evolution within the major kinds. This idea has some similarities to the basic creationist view, for creationism allows for process to occur from the moment of creation and thus for miracle in one sphere to occur contemporaneously with process in another. Furthermore, creationists do not deny that processes of variation occur within the created kinds. Finally, progressive creation denies the essential evolutionary concept that all life has arisen from a single original life-form, itself the product of chance natural occurrences. Progressive creation, however, allows for the geological time-scale within the six-day creation and thus maintains that the fossil record (with its implications of suffering, sudden death and catastrophe) was formed before the creation and Fall of Adam. This is difficult to reconcile with the biblical teaching on the physical effects of the Fall upon an originally perfect creation.

It is appropriate here to clarify the creationist position against a common misunderstanding. In contending that Genesis describes a succession of miraculous creative acts we do not eliminate process from the record. For one thing, of course, natural process must apply to a created object or life-form from the moment of its creation. 'The earth brought forth herb *yielding seed.*' The 'bringing forth' was miraculous, but the yielding of seed was the consequence of natural process. Similarly the created waters would have obeyed the laws of hydrodynamics and hydrostatics from the instant of creation, even *while* other miraculous works were being wrought within their depths, such as the creation of aquatic life. Secondly, process-in-time seems to have been involved in some of the creative acts themselves. Indeed the extension of creation over six days seems to require this. Thus the gathering together of the waters into seas (Genesis 1:9; Psalm 104:6-9) seems to have involved the flow of water under the influence of gravity but, perhaps, at a miraculously reduced viscosity (that is, accelerated speed). We shall see later that no philosophical or theological problem arises from this intermingling of the miraculous with process. This is an important point since many intellectual difficulties and entrenched positions in this debate arise from the problem of harmonizing miracle with nature in a single world-view.

Was evolution God's agency in creation?

We now come to the last of our six areas of conflict, namely the difficulty of reconciling a random amoral process like evolution with the purpose and tenderness attributed to God by the Bible in respect of the physical creation. That the worlds were created for a *purpose* is evident from Revelation 4:11: 'Thou art worthy, O Lord, to receive glory and honour and power: for thou hast created all things, and for thy pleasure they are and were created.' That the worlds were *designed* with intricate care is evident to all who believe in a Creator, both from the testimony of science and from Scripture itself (e.g. Psalm 139:14-16; 19:1; 8:3; 104:1-35; Nehemiah 9:6). That a tenderness characterizes God's attitude towards His created order is clear both from the Psalms already cited and the teachings of Christ Himself ('Your heavenly Father feedeth [the fowls of the air]'; 'Are not two sparrows sold for a farthing? and one of them shall not fall . . . without your Father,' Matthew 6:26; 10:29). Thus purpose and tenderness typify the relationship revealed in Scripture between the Creator and the creature. Evolution stands in such contrast to this picture that it is very difficult to envisage it as God's method of creation. Firstly, of course, evolution appeals to chance processes such as random genetic mutation involving at least ninety-nine *harmful* mutations to every one beneficial mutation. Evolution's 'experiments' therefore give rise to a vast potential for suffering in the animal kingdom for every 'upward' step towards a diversified biosphere. Again, the essential process of natural selection or the 'survival of the fittest' frequently (though not always) involves destructive competition between species. Even the balance of nature as observed today, with its food-chain involving the death of myriads of living creatures, must be an essential part of the evolutionary picture. In contrast the Bible implies that in the original creation only vegetable matter was to be used for food (Genesis 1:29,30; cf. Isaiah 11:6-9) and suggests that the necessity for animal foodstock (Genesis 9:3) arose after the Fall and possibly only after the flood.

The biblical picture, then, is one in which the processes observed today (competition for survival, a carnivorous natural order and harmful genetic mutations) were not present in the 'good' creation as it came from the hand of God. These things, and other features of nature as we know it, arose subsequently as a result of the Fall of man. God did not create the world in 'the bondage of corruption' but 'subjected' it to this condition as a result of Adam's disobedience. The 'whole creation' thus 'groaneth and travaileth in pain' awaiting the consummation of the gospel era and the return of Christ, when it will itself be delivered 'into the glorious liberty of the children of God' (Romans 8:19-23).

If this be the case, it is clear that the processes of neo-Darwinian evolution, *even if* they were shown to be capable today of transforming one species into another, could not have been responsible for the original work of creation. They reflect the consequences of sin rather than the character of the Creator, God's judgemental order rather than His creative means.

Is evolution scientific?

Having discussed in some detail the conflicts which exist between evolution and the Bible, and the impossibility of reconciling the two world-views which they present, we now turn to consider the philosophical objections to evolution as a scientific theory. If evolution cannot be reconciled with Scripture, and if Scripture is true, then evolutionary theory must be at fault.

In order to judge evolution as a scientific doctrine, we must first understand the nature of scientific theory. Too often evolution is presented as 'scientific' and contrasted with the biblical revelation which is a matter of personal belief. We challenge this view, contending that evolution is as much a matter of 'faith' or personal belief as is the creationist viewpoint.

The nature of scientific theory

This subject is discussed elsewhere[2] at greater length and will only be summarized here. First of all, as Karl Popper has emphasized, a theory is only scientific if it can in principle be falsified by scientific study. The law of biogenesis, that is, that life can only be produced by existing living forms and does not arise spontaneously from non-living matter, is a scientific theory in this sense. It is capable of being falsified because a single substantiated instance of spontaneous abiogenesis would suffice to destroy it (or drastically modify it). The theory that the inert gases argon and neon were incapable of chemical combination with other elements was held for many years, but was eventually proved false by the synthesis, under special conditions, of compounds containing some of these atoms. The theory had to be modified to state that *under most conditions* these gases are inert.

Certain categories of statement, however, are not capable of falsification simply because there is no experiment that can be performed which could conceivably prove them false. The claim that Neanderthal man suffered from rickets can be tested scientifically because that disease leaves its marks on the human skeleton. An apparently similar claim that he suffered from epilepsy, however, would not be susceptible to proof or disproof and could not therefore be claimed as a 'scientific' theory, even though epilepsy is just as much a clinical condition as is rickets. The first test, then, of whether a theory is scientific or not lies not in the subject matter of the theory at all, but in the possibility of its proof or disproof.

Thus the claim that life arose once, uniquely, some three thousand million years ago, by the chance combination of inorganic molecules, is not a scientific theory, even though its subject matter (the chemical combination of molecules) appears highly scientific. If the theory claims the past events to be unique, their non-repetition in any scientific experiments performed today cannot, *by definition,* falsify the claim! Thus the theory is not falsifiable and hence not scientific. If, inconceivably, a sterile mixture of chemicals was one day observed to yield a life-form spontaneously, even this would not prove that the same thing happened before the dawn of history, nor that it has not occurred many times since the origin of the earth! The most that can be said is that such a past event is more or less likely to have occurred on the grounds of probability. I have suggested elsewhere[3] that the probability of spontaneous abiogenesis is vanishingly small.

The same argument concerning the falsifiability of theories applies to the evolution of species, that is, to neo-Darwinian evolution. Nothing we can do today is capable of proving that it did not happen. Even in our present situation, where known mechanisms cannot account for or reproduce the evolutionary changes that are alleged to have taken place, it can still be held that natural mechanisms *unknown* to us were at work. Such unfalsifiable theories are not scientific, but are philosophical speculations based upon a naturalistic world-view which interprets all being as a consequence and expression of process.

Secondly, scientific theory exists on all levels of certitude. At one extreme stands the hypothesis, a unifying concept advanced to account for a set of observed facts. At the other end of the spectrum stands the 'law of nature', which is a theory that has passed the test of verification by experiment, has withstood all attempts to falsify it and, in particular, has been successful in correctly predicting the outcome of specially designed experiments. It is possible for a hypothesis to be transformed by experimental study into a law of nature, although this procedure frequently involves modification of the original idea.

Where does evolution stand in the spectrum of scientific 'truth'? Even if we overlook the fundamental problem of its essentially non-scientific nature outlined above, we find that the theory of evolution is really no more than a hypothesis. No experimental verification has emerged from years of study to substantiate the claim that one kind of creature can be transformed into another by (accelerated) mutation and selection. Indeed all the evidence that has accumulated points to a limit to the amount of change that can be induced into any viable population. Our increasing understanding of molecular biology and genetics raises problems for evolutionary theory that Darwin and his early champions could not have envisaged.[21] Experimental palaeontology, with its growing wealth of fossil evidence, is only making more apparent the enormous gaps in the fossil record. As more and more material is unearthed it becomes increasingly obvious that phenotypes intermediate between the major phyla simply did not exist. The missing ancestral types can only be explained either by abandoning conventional neo-Darwinism (as some biologists have done[22]) or by abandoning uniformitarian geology to explain the missing fossil evidence. Evolution then is at best a hypothesis and one that current experimental studies have tended to question rather than substantiate.[23]

Thirdly, a given scientific theory is normally valid within bounds; universal theories are the exception rather than the rule. Thus the laws that describe the motion of a cricket ball are not valid for the motion of an electron nor for that of a galaxy. Any attempt to extrapolate a theory into realms far beyond those in which its validity has been experimentally demonstrated is unscientific. Yet this kind of extrapolation is continually made in evolutionary thinking. Examples are: (a) the doctrine of uniformitarianism, in which even the quantitative rates at which geological processes are observed today are attributed to the past with no objective justification except that of convenience; and (b) the use of natural selection to explain the entire past history of the biosphere, when that process is rarely, if ever, *observed* to produce non-interbreedable populations, let alone entirely new kinds of creature. The evolutionary concept has such enormous appeal as a total world-view that it has been extended to economic, historical, political and religious arenas. Such extravagant extrapolations are, of course, self-evidently unscientific, but they deflect our attention from the vast extrapolations implicit in every attempt to interpret the past history of the physical and biological worlds in evolutionary terms.

Fourthly, scientific theories represent interpretations of

the facts rather than the facts themselves. This important distinction is frequently overlooked and historical evolution is presented as a *fact* rather than a particular interpretation of certain facts, namely the biosphere as observed today and the fossil record. There are alternative interpretations of these facts which are just as respectable scientifically as (some would claim, more so than) the theory of evolution. The fossil record, for instance, is far more consistent with a catastrophic origin than with the gradualism of uniformitarian thinking, since fossils are, demonstrably, not formed in great numbers during slow sedimentation processes such as are typical of our world today. To say that, because there exists a stratified fossil record, then evolution must have occurred, is to confuse the facts of observation with one possible interpretation of those facts, and this is a most unscientific thing to do.

Fifthly, and finally, scientific theories are, at best, only models of reality. Few scientific theories are capable of explaining *all* the facts of observation, although some have been amazingly successful in this respect. Each accepted theory is recognized as providing the best *model*, for the time being, of the reality that underlies certain observable phenomena. When a theory is overthrown, or replaced by a superior theory, the true scientist does not get upset. He recognizes that no violence has been done to reality! It is simply that a particular model has been proved inconsistent with reality and has had to be replaced by a superior one. The proponents of evolution, however, frequently fail to behave in such a scientific manner, becoming emotionally involved when arguments are advanced against the theory. To them the theory has become a reality, a dogma to be defended at all costs. This tendency is frequently found in the writings of evolutionists, is wholly unscientific and actually hinders the progress of science.[24]

The information content of living things

Having reviewed briefly the way in which evolution fails to pass certain tests when viewed as a scientific theory, we now turn to the main philosophical problem raised by the theory. All life as we know it is based upon the genetic code which is itself inscribed upon the DNA molecule. All substances, including DNA, possess what we might call chemical order, which is a direct consequence of the structure of the atoms from which it is formed. This order, for example, determines the bond lengths and angles in molecules and eventually determines the crystallography of solid substances. Here is an order intrinsic to the nature of matter. In DNA, however, and other macromolecules of life (e.g. RNA, proteins), there is superimposed upon this chemical order a higher form of order, namely coded information. A pattern of dots and dashes may exhibit a high degree of order (low entropy) which, however, conveys no meaning. The same dots and dashes arranged according to a certain convention known as the Morse code, may in contrast convey a highly detailed and intelligible message. When we discuss the origin of order in nature, no problem arises from chemical order and pattern. These are properties intrinsic to the nature of matter, properties which are always present, though not always obvious to the naked eye. (Ice possesses a hexagonal crystal structure but this only becomes obvious in the formation of snow flakes. The order is just as present in a block of ice, as X-ray crystallography will demonstrate.) The origin of *coded* order, such as is present in DNA, is quite a different matter, however, since (a) this order is palpably *not* a property of the matter itself and (b) the information content of such codes cannot have developed from random process or 'noise'.

Evolutionists often argue that *any* event, no matter how improbable, must occur given sufficient time. This concept is totally naive, however, as the following illustration will show. A stainless steel pin is a very simple human artefact. It contains atoms of iron, nickel and chromium (plus small amounts of other elements), is homogeneous and very simply shaped. Its degree of complexity is minute compared with the simplest life-form known to science. It does however have the attribute of bearing elementary 'information', namely it has a sharp end and a blunt end. We use the term 'information' because these aspects of shape cannot arise from the intrinsic properties of the material of which it is composed. They are imposed upon the base material by design. A sphere could occur naturally, as could certain other shapes, but only deliberate tooling or a mould could impart the particular, improbable shape of an ordinary pin. Would an evolutionist insist that somewhere on earth there exists a stainless steel pin which has arisen by natural process? Yet the probability of such an event is almost infinitely greater than that of the first DNA molecule or protein molecule arising by chance.[21]

Thus the origin of code, or genetic language, on which all life processes are based, represents an enormous problem for those who attribute biogenesis to normal chemical process. Even though it represents a reduction of entropy, it is quite possible for a polymer to arise chemically; but not a *coded* polymer. A simple analogy is that a clay 'tablet' might readily be produced by natural process, but a clay tablet *with writing on it,* if found, would immediately be recognized as the work of an intelligent hand. The creationist's argument is not that systems of greatly reduced entropy could not arise by chance, but that the particular *kind* of entropy reduction represented by the genetic code could not have come about without the participation of intelligence.

The theistic evolutionist, of course, unlike his materialistic colleague, is able to concede that God was providing just such an intelligent 'input' during the development of life. But this admission really undermines the whole evolutionary position because it means that the natural processes of physics and chemistry could not have *themselves* brought about the creation of life. And if God's intervention in those processes (miracle?) is a condition of creation, how does this differ from the concept of special creation? There is thus a built-in contradiction within theistic evolution. It is a self-inconsistent doctrine. For evolution is no longer evolution once any non-natural agency is introduced as a condition for its operation. The essence of the evolutionary concept is that present natural process can account for the entire geosphere and biosphere and, once this essence is denied, evolution collapses.

It is important here to distinguish between miracle and providence. By miracles we mean actual physical events which could not have happened in the way they did by the operation of natural process. A miracle thus involves the suspension or replacement of physical laws. By providence we signify God's control and use of natural process to achieve His purposes. The theistic evolutionist must specify which of these distinct alternatives he has in mind when he claims that God 'used' or 'overruled' evolution to effect His creative purposes. If he means that God so controlled molecular processes that events took place that otherwise would have occurred only with vanishing probability, he is appealing to the miraculous. This involves the objections mentioned above. If, on the other hand, he means that there was a finite probability of life emerging (and diversifying) by natural process, then God's involvement was a providential one, namely of ensuring that such natural process *did* occur and that, out of a variety of *naturally possible* courses of development, one was chosen that subserved His will. If this is the stance adopted, it makes nonsense of the distinction between God's constant providence (from which surely He has never ceased or rested) and His creative work (which was 'ended' on the seventh day). I frankly cannot see any way out of this dilemma for the theory of theistic evolution. Either the miraculous has to be invoked, in which case the events cannot be ascribed to 'evolution', or else only providence is involved in which case the biblical teaching on creation is negated.

Scientific riddles unsolved by evolution

It is not my purpose in this chapter to become involved in the scientific, as opposed to philosophical and biblical arguments against evolution. These have been dealt with elsewhere.[3,23,25] There are a number of areas, however, where the distinction between scientific and philosophical considerations becomes blurred and for the sake of completeness we therefore enumerate several of the problems that evolution fails to solve. We are not concerned here with matters that can obviously be resolved by dint of further scientific research, but rather those stubborn areas of speculation that by their nature are unlikely to yield to physical investigation. What follows is simply an enumeration and not a detailed discussion.
a. Chemical evolution or abiogenesis. The present theory requires that the earth originally possessed a reducing atmosphere, yet there is no proof of this contention and several contra-indications (for example, the highly oxygenated character of the earth's crustal rock and the rapid production of oxygen from water vapour in U.V. light with removal of

hydrogen from earth's gravity). If life *did* evolve in a reducing atmosphere and if our present oxygen derived only from photosynthesis, there should be fossil evidence of anaerobic, photosynthesizing plant life. Yet none exists. The assumption of a reducing atmosphere therefore remains a philosophical presupposition which is unlikely ever to be provable or falsifiable.

b. The polymerization of proteins and/or DNA would have required either anhydrous conditions or special catalytic molecules. In either case it must remain a matter of speculation whether the appropriate conditions ever existed. The argument that they *must* have existed, because *otherwise* life could not have arisen by natural process, begs the question completely and underlines the essentially philosophical nature of the theory of chemical evolution. (Philosophy proceeds on the basis of axiom, science on the basis of experimental observation.)

c. The enormous step of *forming the first living cell* would have involved processes of molecular self-organization unknown to science. Furthermore the complex mechanism of cellular reproduction must have evolved in the *brief period of viability* of the first protocell. No way in which this could have occurred is known. Again, acceptance that this occurred by natural process is an act of stupendous faith on the part of the evolutionist.

d. Neo-Darwinian evolution. The adequacy of the proposed mechanisms to account for macro-evolution is doubted by many biologists[22] and remains experimentally unverified. Natural selection, in particular, would normally be expected to produce convergence rather than divergence in populations.[3] In so far as natural selection is claimed to cause divergence, convergence or static situations according to circumstances, it is difficult to see how such a non-specific factor could have produced the inexorable 'upward' progress of the biosphere claimed by evolution.

e. The fossil record. The very existence of this record is more consistent with a catastrophic origin[26] than with a uniformitarian one, quite apart from those specific remains which indicate formation by sudden inundations of vast extent.[27] The rates of sedimentation used to date the geological column are the low rates characteristic of the deep oceans whereas it is obvious that all but marine fossils were formed on or near land.

The absence of simple and intermediate forms in the fossil record is a constant embarrassment to evolution. The usual answer is to offer a few homologous series to show progressive evolution within a kind (for example, the celebrated evolutionary sequence of the horse). This answer is quite unsatisfactory because the selection of fossils to arrange in a homologous series is a subjective matter resting on the evolutionary presuppositions of the researcher, for example, the assumption that the evolution of the horse involved a gradual increase in size.[28] Secondly, the existence of a few supposed homologous series of fossils in no way explains the interphylatic gaps; indeed, if anything, it serves only to emphasize them!

The evolution of one specialized organism from another specialized form is difficult to envisage. Rather we should expect a generalized common ancestor.[3] Such generalized forms, which should form the trunk and main branches of the 'tree of evolution', are notable for their absence.

Although these various comments on the fossil record are 'scientific', the methods adopted by evolutionary theory to circumvent the problems raised are decidedly philosophical. The insistence that the fossil record was formed slowly over thousands of millions of years is based upon the presupposition of uniformitarian geology. The homologous series are constructed as proof of gradual development working on the *prior assumption* that the remains must be related by evolutionary succession. The gaps are dismissed by the claim that the fossil record is incomplete, a claim based squarely on the assumption that gradual transitions *did* (in spite of the evidence) occur between the major phyla! It is not my purpose here to minimize the difficulties facing research into remotely historical events, but to show that evolution habitually employs circular argument to prove its case *without acknowledging the fact.*

Creation and science: a synthesis

The reader might well ask, 'Having rejected theistic evolution, what alternative view of creation can you offer which is wholly consistent with the biblical record and with the facts of modern scientific observation?' It is my purpose in this final section to attempt to answer that question. I have suggested several times that one of the basic problems for many people is that of reconciling the miraculous with providence on the one hand and modern science on the other. I believe that theistic evolution, progressive creation and many of the ideas associated with these views are espoused by Christians, consciously or unconsciously, in an attempt to solve this basic dilemma. Consequently, our task of constructing a worldview which is both biblical and scientifically acceptable needs to begin with these basic matters rather than with the creation story.

A theology of science

I have suggested elsewhere the urgent need for a theological framework in which to set the methods and findings of modern science. Without such a 'theology of science', the conflict between science and religion remains both unresolved *and* ill-defined. Thus to better understand the past relationship between God and His created universe, we begin by examining their present relationship. In Colossians 1:15-19 we find this relationship defined. Of course, this is a *Christocentric* passage having as its main purpose the establishment of the coequality of Christ and the Father. But it is exactly this design on the part of the apostle which makes the passage so valuable for our purpose because in identifying the attributes of God shared by Christ, the writer cannot omit the question of the creation and sustenance of the material universe. 'By him [Christ] ', declares Paul, 'were all things created, that are in heaven and that are in earth, visible and invisible . . . all things were created by him, and for him.' Thus the apostle repeats the assertion of the prologue to John's Gospel, concerning the agency in creation of the Second Person of the triune God. But Paul continues, 'And he is before all things, and by him all things consist.' This verse emphasizes Christ's precedence, both in time and status, over the whole created order, but it also states explicitly the dependent relationship that exists between Him and the physical world. 'By him all things consist,' — that is, hold together. ·The integrity of the material realm is a derived integrity. It consists not so much in the intrinsic properties of matter and energy but in the present-tense being of the Deity.

In scientific terms, of course, we would say that 'all things hold together' by the operation of physical law, but we do not deceive ourselves into thinking that the laws of science are the efficacious *cause* of the integrity of nature. We recognize that the laws are simply our *description* of the manner in which the universe functions. The true *cause* of the forces and natural processes described by scientific law lies beyond the realm of scientific investigations. We do not, as scientists, speculate why masses attract one another, nor why the law of gravity is an inverse square law rather than, say, an inverse cube law. We simply accept nature as we find it, and attempt to describe its myriad phenomena in laws as few and as general as may be possible. In doing so we discover a mathematical harmony and order about creation that is positively aesthetic in its appeal, namely the element of 'design'. The fact that science reveals a category of order in nature that our *human minds are capable of appreciating* is, of course, evidence that creation is the product of an intelligence not wholly dissimilar to our own.

Returning to Colossians 1:17, then, we may conclude that scientific law is a description of the manner in which Christ upholds and sustains the natural order. We do not limit this work to the natural universe, since the context clearly embraces non-material entities among the 'all things' which consist in Him. It is equally clear, however, that the physical creation is very much in the writer's mind as he identifies Christ as the source of all being.

Unlike creation, which is a past, accomplished work (Colossians 1:16: 'were created'), the sustaining power of Christ is a present and continuous activity. This, moreover, is a more fundamental activity than that normally delineated by the term 'providence'. Providence is described elsewhere by the same apostle in these terms: 'All things work together for good to them that love God . . .' (Romans 8:28). Of course, providence is not limited to the believer, and in that sense this verse does not define it fully, but the distinction I wish to draw is between the two clauses, 'all things consist', and 'all things work'. The first clause surely refers to the very *constitution* of things while the second refers to their *operation* or function. Thus God's employment of ravens to feed Elijah was providential; the fact that such things as ravens existed to be so employed is the burden of Colossians 1:17.

A second New Testament Scripture may now be cited to reinforce what we have stated so far, namely Hebrews 1:1-3. This passage is remarkably similar to Colossians 1:15-19, having the same Christological purpose, and identifying Christ as God's agent 'by whom also he made the worlds'. Verse 2 continues, 'Who being the brightness of [God's] glory, and the express image of his person, and upholding all things by the word of his power . . .'

This last clause expresses in different words the same ideas as Colossians 1:17, namely that 'all things' are upheld or sustained by the ever-present activity of God. An added thought appears in this verse, namely that Christ imparts integrity to the material universe by the 'word of His power'. Here lies the effectual cause of those material interactions and processes described and employed by science. The source of, say, the binding energy of the atom, is the power of God. Material energy is derived from pure spiritual energy. This concept is necessary of course to account for the initial creation *ex nihilo,* but our verse suggests that God's spiritual power not only originated matter and energy, but sustains it in existence and controls its interactions and processes.

The full expression 'the word of His power' is surely intended to convey purpose or intention. He upholds all things not just by His power, but by a deliberate putting forth or exercise of that power. God is the *active* source of being, not just a passive 'ground of existence'. This adds new point to Paul's famous declaration that 'In him we live, and move, and have our being' (Acts 17:28). God is active, sentient, purposeful in His upholding and sustaining of the physical worlds. This final point is vital as we come now to examine the question of miracles.

Miracles

By definition, a miracle involves the suspension or replacement of natural process and physical law. For the time required for the miracle to take place, rules other than the normal physical laws govern and control events. Thus Christ's first miracle, in which water was turned into wine, conceivably involved the transformation of some atoms of oxygen into atoms of carbon followed by the assembly of sugar and other large molecules. None of these nuclear or chemical transformations would have occurred naturally under the conditions prevailing, and they must therefore have taken place under rules unknown to science which temporarily prevailed over normal scientific law. (We do not here concern ourselves with 'miracles of timing' in which natural processes are used by God to realize His purposes. Such miracles really fall under the heading of providence rather than the miraculous.)

Now we have maintained earlier that the normal laws of physics and chemistry are the moment-by-moment expression of God's will, the ever-present 'word of his power', the contemporaneous expression of His purpose. If this is so, the suspension or replacement of those laws becomes a very straightforward matter. God simply changes His 'instructions' to nature in such a manner and for such a period as is required for the miracle to be performed. Thus if the normal laws of physics require that oxygen atoms are stable and do not decay spontaneously into carbon atoms, such spontaneous decay, without release of catastrophic energy, may be brought about by a momentary change in the rules governing the stability of oxygen atoms. Since the normal rules are simply the present-tense expression of God's will, the extraordinary rules which momentarily supervene are also of this same nature. No inconsistency arises in God's mind or action; there is no arbitrary 'intervention' by God into the natural order; miracles are not amoral.

Creation

Let us now, as briefly as possible, apply these ideas to creation and providence. This we will do in outline only and the reader is referred elsewhere for a fuller statement.[3]

The *ex nihilo* creation, a concept unique to the Judaeo-Christian tradition, was an event in which matter and energy, space and time, together with the laws or principles that describe the structure and behaviour of these entities, were inaugurated from a purely spiritual source. Following this event, and in a period which is not necessarily limited by Scripture, the heaven and earth (that is, the whole universe) were formed. At some juncture the earth is recorded as existing 'without form and void'. Although miracle was obviously necessary for the origin of energy and matter, we accept that subsequent event leading to the 'formless' earth may have occurred by miracle, natural process or an admixture of the two, since Scripture gives us no certain guidance on this matter. The scene from this point in the creation narrative is earth itself.

The formlessness and emptiness of the earth at this stage have been variously interpreted but we adopt the simple view that formlessness denoted an absence of geographical feature rather than a conceptually difficult idea of *shapelessness.* The entire surface of the globe was covered by an ocean which merged upwards into an atmosphere of water vapour and other gases. The reference to the Spirit of God moving on the waters is obscure but suggests a spiritual presence preparatory to the creative acts that follow. Again the Scripture seems not to allow us the liberty to separate the material world from God's spiritual presence, as if they were non-interacting entities. Rather do we find here an unabashed intermingling of nature and the work of God. The Bible writers were not inhibited in their thinking by such philosophical systems as naturalism, dualism or even complementarity.

Space will not permit us here to rehearse the details of the creation week. We take the view, however, that each repetition of the words: 'And God said . . .' introduces a new miraculous fiat in which events occurred which required the suspension or replacement of natural law. This applies not only to the obviously miraculous assembly of atoms and molecules (dust) into living organisms of various kinds, but also to events which could conceivably have happened by natural process.

Thus the first light on earth *could* have dawned by the clearing of a dense atmosphere, by completely natural means. It could equally have appeared as a result of a *miraculous* clearing of such an atmosphere. This second alternative is just as much a miracle as that involved in the idea that Genesis 1:3 describes the first creation of light anywhere in the universe. Similarly, to suggest that the fourth day witnessed the *appearance* of sun, moon and stars in the sky rather than their creation (which is then set in verse 1) is not to diminish in any respect the belief that this appearance involved a miraculous act (in which the veil of cloud, if such there was, became dispersed). What may at first seem to be a watering down of the miraculous element of Genesis 1 is nothing of the kind. These particular interpretations of the illumination of the earth and of the fourth day are preferred because they furnish the passage with a greater *internal* consistency, not because they make the fiat miracles any less miraculous and 'easier' to accept.

The alternation of day and night, following the first dawn, together with the separation of day from night seem to describe nothing other than the natural phenomena familiar to us today. Here, then, is natural process at work as a backcloth to the creative miracles which populate the six successive days. Indeed, to deny that the days of Genesis 1 are normal days not only offends the context but also banishes natural process from the record! At this point it is the creationist who insists on natural process and the theistic evolutionist who will not allow it! Into this scenario of physical process are injected the successive creative acts. No duration in real time is required for a miracle, though equally there is no law that requires miracles to be instantaneous! All we know is that, by replacement of physical laws as required, God caused the recorded events to be completed in the times specified. Once we have grasped the nature of miracle, this should cause no intellectual or philosophical difficulties.

The miraculous creation of man is attested by two distinct arguments. Genesis 2:7 states that God formed man directly from the 'dust' in the same manner as He formed the animals. This seems to exclude the formation of Adam from *already viable species*. Furthermore, the second half of the same verse indicates that a special act of vivification was required ('man became a living soul': by common consent, soul does not signify a spiritual dimension but simply a living organism). Such vitalization would be quite unnecessary had Adam evolved from existing primates. Secondly, whatever one makes of the account of woman's creation from one of Adam's 'sides', the New Testament explains that there was a temporal order in their creation ('Adam was first formed, then Eve'—1 Timothy 2:13). This again excludes the evolutionary transformation of an existing population of apes into *homo sapiens,* since man and woman would then have necessarily evolved simultaneously.

Providence

The subject of providence has arisen several times in the course of this essay. We saw that theistic evolution blurs the distinction between creation and providence and is also inconsistent in equating with providence God's imagined use of evolution as a creative agency. Providence is distinct from miracle in that it involves no suspension or replacement of natural process but rather the use of such process to achieve particular aims.

The subject of providence is a large one, both biblically and philosophically. It involves questions of the sovereignty of God in human affairs, the permitted occurrence of evil and suffering and the matter of free will and determinism. It is not therefore a subject that can be developed here except to emphasize the very real differences between providence and creation which are confused or ignored by theistic evolution.

Of course, there is a continuity between creation and providence, as illustrated in Psalm 104 where a poetic account of creation (vv.1-9) passes naturally into a hymn of praise to God for His providential care over the things created. Did God create the grass and the herb? Then also he 'causeth the grass to grow for the cattle, and herb for the service of man' (v.14). Did he create the dry land? Then also 'the high hills are a refuge for the wild goats; and the rocks for conies' (v.18). Nevertheless, in spite of this obvious continuity, the Bible's distinction between a past, completed creation (Genesis 2:1-2; Job 38:4; Psalm 104:5; John 1:1-3; Hebrews

1:2) and a present continuing providence is too self-evident to avoid. It is not possible, therefore, to ascribe 'creation' to providence, for the former involves the miraculous while the latter does not. To attribute creation to the overruling or direction of statistically determined events (which is an alternative definition of providence) is to apply the doctrine of uniformitarianism to the realm of God's activities, that is, to claim that God always acted in the past as He acts in the present. This is palpably unbiblical, for the progressive nature of God's dealings with the world and the human race, involving a miraculous origin and an equally miraculous culmination (for example, the resurrection of the dead) are undeniable if we believe the Bible at all.

Conclusion

Let us finally, therefore, draw together the threads of this discussion. We have argued against evolution on biblical grounds, citing six areas of conflict between the scriptural and evolutionary accounts of creation. These areas concerned the questions of time-scale, the finished nature of creation, the Fall and its physical consequences, the plurality of the creative fiats, the inadequacy of natural process to account for the origin of the biosphere and the moral problems associated with the idea of evolution as an agency of divine creation. We then moved on to discuss the philosophical shortcomings of evolution, applying a variety of tests to the claim that it is a *bona fide* scientific theory. We saw that, at best, it is a scientific hypothesis and that many of its assertions are, in fact, philosophical rather than scientific, being based on axioms rather than observations. Finally, we have seen that the Bible itself provides us with a key to the understanding of science and miracles, and that, using this key, we are able to accept the obvious historical interpretation of the Genesis creation story without doing violence to a proper view of science and natural process.

Perhaps the most important point we have argued is that Christians must adopt a biblical view of science and process and not borrow from extra-biblical philosophy a theory of science which rigorously excludes such biblical ingredients as the occurrence of miracles and the subjection of natural process to the will of God. If we were more robustly scriptural in our evaluation of science, we would be less inclined to be mesmerized by the tenuous logic, circular reasoning and leaps of faith which characterize the general theory of evolution.

References

1. Andrews, E.H., in *The Bible under attack,* Evangelical Press, Welwyn, 1978, p.52.
2. Andrews, E.H., *Is evolution scientific?,* Evangelical Press, Welwyn, 1977.
3. Andrews, E.H., *From nothing to nature,* Evangelical Press, Welwyn, 1978.
4. Jones, H.R., in *The Bible under attack,* Evangelical Press, Welwyn, 1978, pp.9-26.
5. Young, D.A., *Creation and the flood,* Baker Book House, Grand Rapids, 1977, pp.17-22.
6. Buswell, J.O., *A systematic theology of the Christian religion,* Zondervan, Grand Rapids, 1962, p.140.
7. Davies, J.D., *Dictionary of the Bible,* Philadelphia, 1898, p.147.
8. Noordtzij, A., *Gods Woord en der Eeuwen Getuigenis,* Kampen: J.H. Kok, 1924.
9. Ridderbos, N.H., *Beschouwingen over Genesis I,* Kampen: J.H. Kok, 1963.
10. Kline, M.G., 'Because it had not rained', *Westminster Theological Journal,* 20, 1958, 146-157.
11. Young, E.J., *Studies in Genesis one,* Presbyterian and Reformed Publishing Co., Philadelphia, 1964, pp.43-76.
12. Young, D.A., *op. cit.,* pp.23-41.
13. Ramm, B., *The Christian view of science and Scripture,* Paternoster Press, London, 1955, p.164.
14. Buswell, J.O., *op. cit.,* pp.133-147.
15. Young, D.A., *op. cit.,* pp.81-89.
16. Fields, W.W., *Unformed and unfilled,* Presbyterian and Reformed Publishing Co., Nutley, N.J., 1976.
17. Fields, W.W., *op. cit.,* pp.168-179.

18. Wiseman, P.J., *Clues to creation in Genesis,* Marshall, Morgan and Scott, 1977.
19. Morris, H.M., *The Genesis record,* Evangelical Press, Welwyn, 1977, p.127.
20. Ramm, B., *op. cit.,* p.76.
21. Wilder-Smith, A.E., *The creation of life,* Harold Shaw Publishers, Wheaton, Illinois, 1970.
22. Grasse, P.P., *Evolution of living organisms,* Academic Press, New York, 1970.
23. Klotz, J.W., *Genes, Genesis and evolution,* Concordia, St Louis, 1955.
24. Thompson, W.R., Introduction to *The origin of species,* Everyman Library, No. 811, 1956.
25. Gish, D.T., *Evolution. The fossils say no!,* Creation-Life Publishers, San Diego, 1973.
26. Whitcomb, J.C., Jr and Morris, H.M., *The Genesis flood,* Presbyterian and Reformed Publishing Co., Philadelphia, p.497, (fossils).
27. Velikovsky, I., *Earth in upheaval,* Sphere Books Ltd., London, 1973, pp.3-10.
28. Monty White, A.J., *What about origins?* Dunestone Printers Ltd, Newton Abbot, 1978, p.123.

CHAPTER SIX

One of the major arguments in favour of evolution is the enormous time-scale permitted for its operation by historical geology, according to which the earth is 4,500 million years old. It is not an absolute requirement of special creation that the earth be young (that is, tens of thousands of years rather than thousands of millions). But the biblical record nevertheless appears to be at odds with the vast scale currently accepted for geological time and it is appropriate therefore that the evidence for great age should be re-examined. Our conclusion is not clear-cut but does raise considerable doubts about the validity of the accepted geochronology, whether based upon stratigraphical or radiometric determinations. It is not therefore necessary, in the writer's view, to abandon the biblical implications of a young earth under the weight of geological evidence.

The age of the earth

Introduction

Before we become involved with detailed argument, I believe it is important to step back a little to survey the matters at issue between those who subscribe to uniformitarian geology and those who believe the earth is relatively young. In order to do so I want to introduce an illustration.

Suppose one morning I go into the garden and find a fine ripe apple lying on the ground beneath my prize apple tree. The most probable explanation is that the apple is a windfall, dislodged from its branch by a gust of wind or even a passing bird. Although this is the most likely explanation, however, it is not the only *possible* one. For example, the apple might have been deliberately picked by a mischievous boy and taken home. Before he could consume it, however, his mother discovered what had happened and sent him back to replace the apple under the tree.

The 'windfall theory' is the more probable theory, simply because it requires only a single unobserved event. The 'small boy theory' requires a succession of interlocking events which are equally unobserved. The intrinsic probability of a theory reduces as the number of assumptions (unobserved events) which have to be invoked increases.

It is a general principle of modern science (derived from 'Occam's razor') that the explanation requiring the smallest number of assumptions should always be adopted. Although this explanation is seldom the only possible one, it is nevertheless the most probable and thus (by definition) the most 'true'. Thus a scientific mind would accept the 'windfall theory' rather than the 'small boy theory' to explain the fallen apple.

Uniformitarian geology is, without question, an attractive theory of the history of the earth because it involves a minimum number of assumptions. It posits, for example, a steady-state model of the earth, requiring no assumptions regarding past unobserved catastrophes. It does not need to invoke unobserved processes (whether natural or miraculous) occurring at some past era but unknown to us today. Like the 'windfall theory', it presents itself as the most probable, and therefore the truest, the most scientific explanation of terrestrial history.

Let us, however, return to the orchard. Suppose now that I examine the fallen apple closely and observe the imprint of a set of small human teeth. This additional evidence dramatically alters the picture. Now the 'small boy theory' immediately assumes a much greater relative probability, since the 'windfall theory' *although requiring fewer assumptions* is unable to account for all the facts of observation. We must always select the simplest explanation of a phenomenon, but never to the exclusion of some of the evidence. The most probable (truest) scientific theory is that which explains *all* the facts of observation in the simplest manner.

Standing, Newton-like, beneath our apple tree, we are forced to make a choice. Either we must reject the 'windfall theory', despite its simplicity (scientists would say 'elegance'), and accept that only a more complicated explanation will suffice. Or else we may insist that the teeth marks can somehow be reconciled with the 'windfall' theory. We might say, 'Yes, admittedly they look like teeth marks, but that would contradict the "windfall theory" so the marks cannot be what they seem. They are probably punctures caused by marauding wasps or ants which just happen to resemble teeth marks.' Thus we reinterpret the teeth marks to make them consistent with the 'windfall theory'. Our guiding principle is that an elegant theory, which explains so much so simply, must at all costs be retained.

Two kinds of teeth marks

The creationist's complaint about uniformitarian geology is not that it lacks elegance or plausibility, but that it considerably over-simplifies the issue by ignoring or explaining away the contrary evidence (the teeth marks). This contrary evidence is of two kinds. Firstly, there is the scientific evidence that militates against uniformitarian geology, for example, the widespread evidence of past geological catastrophe and of processes (like mass fossilization) not observable today. The other kind of 'teeth mark' is the testamentary evidence of Scripture which, taken at its face value, teaches that the earth is young.

Of course, the uniformitarian thinker accepts that catastrophic events have occurred in the past, and that the planet's crust today is more quiescent than of old. But at the same time he refuses to allow these 'teeth marks' to affect his basic viewpoint. He dismisses any violent episodes of geological history as mere perturbations of uniform process and thus as irrelevant to the mainstream of geological morphogenesis. The biblical testimony is treated in a similar fashion. Instead of admitting the Genesis record as evidence bearing on the actual history of the earth, he reinterprets these 'teeth marks' to harmonize them with uniformitarian time-scales, even though, as we have discussed elsewhere in this volume, such 'harmonization' involves a plethora of special pleadings and does violence to the text.

It is the writer's view that we must squarely face the situation that the biblical testimony and the uniformitarian model of geological history stand in contradiction. I will go further to agree that there are many geological observations that are *better* explained (in our present state of knowledge) by the conventional geological theories and that are difficult to reconcile with the model of a young earth. In many ways uniformitarianism remains the 'most probable' explanation in the sense that the 'windfall theory' is more probable than the 'small boy theory' in our illustration. In spite of this, I believe that to cling to conventional wisdom in this matter, and to explain away the teeth marks of contrary evidence, is a failure to observe scientific methodology which requires that *all* the evidence be allowed its full weight. If this leads to an impasse or antinomy, so be it. Just as the contradictory theories of the wave and corpuscular natures of light had to be reconciled by a transcendent concept (that of quantum mechanics), so perhaps the contradictions here discussed may have to be resolved on a higher plane.

In the remainder of this chapter, therefore, I want to look first at the scientific case against uniformitarian geology and its time-scale, and secondly at the possible solutions that may exist on a transcendent level (both scientific and miraculous).

Scientific arguments against uniformitarianism

Let me admit immediately that this is an area in which the proponents of a young earth tend to be on the defensive. This, however, should not be interpreted as indicating any weakness in their case, but rather that professional geologists, who have the facts at their fingertips, are likely by their very training to be espoused to conventional thinking in this field. Thus Young,[1] in a recent book recommending the 'day-age' theory of progressive creationism, constantly complains of the problems he would face in the practice of his geological profession, if he were forced to accept the mature creation theory.

The arguments for an ancient earth (approximately 4,500 million years is the current estimate) fall into three main categories. First come the arguments from cosmogony, involving the length of time required for the earth to form from interstellar matter. I do not intend to deal with this (except later in broad terms) because we really have no agreed theory of planetary formation and thus no acceptable model on which to base our arguments. The second category of evidence concerns the rates of formation of sedimentary rocks and other geological processes such as mountain-building and continental drift. The third type of evidence is that of radiometric dating. Let us consider the two latter areas in turn.

Rate processes

A 'rate process' is one which requires the passage of time for its accomplishment. The flow of heat and the deformation of fluids and solids are typical rate processes. One of the all-pervading aspects of rate processes is that the time required for a given event or transition to take place is strongly dependent upon environmental factors such as temperature and pressure. An exception to this appears to be the radioactive decay rates of unstable isotopes, which seem to be independent of most environmental factors, but even this has been questioned recently.[2] Furthermore, any bombardment of such atoms by energetic particles can vastly increase decay rates as in a nuclear reactor or atomic bomb.

The problem therefore in assigning rates to unobserved historical processes is vast; indeed it is almost insoluble. Unless we can also assign values to the temperature, the forces that were acting, the chemical environment and so forth, it is impossible to be specific about the rate at which a given process occurred in the past. And, moreoever, the differences are not small. In the deformation of solids by plastic flow, and in the flow of simple liquids, as well as in chemical reactions, the rate of the process depends exponentially upon the temperature. Thus, if a certain rise in temperature produces a tenfold increase in the rate of a process, an additional temperature rise of the same amount will increase the rate to a hundred times its original value. A third increment of temperature rise multiplies the rate to a thousand times the starting value and so on. Of course other events often intervene to complicate this simple picture, but the point I want to make is that processes involving chemical reaction, deformation, flow and so on can vary in rate by orders of magnitude depending on the temperature at which they occur.

Now geologists frequently appeal (correctly in my view) to great temperature changes to account for past geological events. Metamorphic rock formations are the most obvious example, in which the temperature rise was sufficient to cause crystal phase transformations including melting and recrystallization. Under such conditions the rock would have become extremely plastic and capable of high rates of deformation. Mountain ranges could be formed on the time-scale of days rather than millennia *given* sufficiently high temperatures. Equally, non-metamorphic, sedimentary rocks could undergo rapid deformations if their lithification were incomplete. Everything depends upon the conditions prevailing at the time.

Similar considerations apply to the effect of forces on rates of deformation, erosion, deposition and so on. Thus the process of sand-blasting, in which sand particles are projected at a surface by compressed air, can accomplish in minutes a degree of erosion that might take centuries to occur by normal wind-blown grit. In the same way, jet aircraft canopies may suffer surface erosion by droplets of rain that would cause no damage whatever to a stationary object. We have all seen the amount of silt and debris that can be deposited by a flash flood in minutes, corresponding to the deposition of years under normal water-flow conditions.

Against these rather self-evident considerations it is sometimes argued that high rates of deformation in rock strata would cause fracture rather than deformation and folding as observed. Thus mountain-building must be an intrinsically slow process. But this only follows under certain conditions. If, for example, a hydrostatic pressure is applied to a brittle material, it may eventually become ductile, or, in other words, it flows rather than fractures. Even without this type of 'all-round' pressure, many solids are brittle in tension but ductile in compression, so that under compressive loads they actually flow. Furthermore, of course, much depends upon the degree of lithification of a sediment. If it is still relatively 'soft' when deformed, the likelihood of flow without fracture is greatly enhanced, as also is the likely rate of erosion.

Another argument by which rates of rock formation are sometimes deduced involves the internal morphology of the strata. Thus water ripples in sandy deposits, or the segregation of larger from smaller particles, do indeed give some indication of the conditions under which sedimentation occurred. But a given morphology does not correspond to a unique rate of formation. Rather, it corresponds to a *set of conditions* in which sedimentation rate is only one of several variables. Other important variables will be the flow-rate of water, its density, and its viscosity. Thus, while some information can certainly be derived from morphology it seems quite unsafe to deduce that morphological similarities between past and present sediments necessarily imply equal rates of deposition.

Using rate processes to date the rocks

From what has gone before, it is clear that we have insufficient knowledge about the conditions under which historical geological processes took place to allow us, with any confidence, to ascribe quantative rates to them. Uniformitarian doctrine therefore makes an *arbitrary* assumption that geological process is, in the main, in a steady state. It is agreed that this is the simplest assumption to make and, in the absence of contrary evidence, a reasonable one. This does not, however, remove the arbitrary nature of the assumption and we must recognize that the steady-state model of uniformitarian geology is just that, a *model* based upon simplifying assumptions. The geological time-scale that emerges from this model is thus a *model* time-scale and has a relative but not an absolute validity.

To emphasize this point further we may cite the calculation of rock ages based on sedimentation rates. In this calculation the maximum thicknesses of all the strata in the geological column are taken. The argument is that the true depth of any deposit corresponds at least to the maximum thickness observed anywhere on earth. Where the particular stratum is shallow, or absent, this is attributed to erosion or simply the absence of deposition. As a result, a virgin geological column is constructed having a phanerozoic thickness of some 500,000 feet, about ten times the thickness actually observed anywhere on earth. The total thickness of the virgin geological column is now divided by a fixed deposition rate to give the age of the deepest sediment. Which particular deposition rate is chosen? A very slow one, corresponding to the sedimentation rates estimated today for the deep oceans, far from the silt-laden waters of the continental shelf. Surely an *average* sedimentation rate would have been more appropriate? But even more bizarre is the fact that many of the sediments concerned contain, and are indexed by, the fossils of land-based and shallow water organisms which must have been buried at the much higher sedimentation rates appropriate to continental run-offs. The depth of silt required to bury a ten-foot dinosaur would have taken 10,000 years to accumulate at deep ocean rates. Indeed it is hard to imagine any significant fossilization process occurring at the assumed rates of one foot in a thousand years, since complete burial in a very short time is normally a pre-condition of effective fossilization. Further evidence of rapid deposition comes from polystrate fossils, such as tree trunks which penetrate several strata and show that tens of feet of rock were laid down in very short periods of time. In short, the ages of rocks calculated from sedimentation rates are at best arbitrary relative to real time, and at worst strongly biased to give improbably great ages. It is true that geologists today recognize that sedimentation is a complex process and that uniformitarian assumptions are crude. My argument is, however, that the accepted geological time-scale was originally 'fixed' by just such crude assumptions and has not been recalculated to take account of the complexity of the sedimentation process. Indeed, it is doubtful whether *any* age estimate based upon sedimentation rates would be accepted today if it were advanced for the first time!

My uniformitarian friends will protest vigorously that I am being unfair. They will say that sedimentation rate calculations were never intended to give absolute ages and that my criticisms are rendered innocuous by the fact that the traditional geological time-scale under discussion here has been verified within relatively small margins of error by the absolute methods of radiochronology. We must examine this claim presently, but if we assume it to be true, it only makes matters worse. Granted that sedimentation calculations are demonstrably *arbitrary,* how is it that radiometric dating confirms them as basically accurate? Is this not a surprising result? If I mark off a hundred equal but arbitrary divisions along a strip of wood, it is most unlikely that the total length will come to one metre. I might be two or three times, even ten times, too short or too long. It would be a great coincidence if truly arbitrary divisions turned out to be just one centimetre in length.

I am not here accusing anyone of fraud! But I do believe that in adopting the various assumptions necessary in radiometric dating, experimenters have, consciously or unconsciously, taken the existing geological time-scale as a calibrating yardstick, tending to reject as untrustworthy any results that differ from it significantly. Documented evidence of this attitude is given later.

I have pointed out elsewhere[3] that equally realistic assumptions, using sedimentation rates appropriate to flood and inundation conditions on or near land, would dramatically reduce the supposed age of the geological column (to tens of thousands of years instead of thousands of millions). Morris[4] has listed over seventy rate processes observable today, together with the age of the earth (or universe) deduced from them on the basis of uniformitarian assumptions, that is, that the rates were historically constant. The age estimates obtained vary from less than a few thousand years to five hundred million years. For example, calculations based on the influx of various elements to the oceans via rivers give ages as diverse as 100 years (aluminium), 8000-9000 years (nickel, silicon) and 260 million years (sodium). It is obvious of course that in many cases the uniformitarian assumptions are invalid and the age obtained fictitious. Our problem is, however, to decide *which* uniformitarian assumptions are correct and which are false. I do not think that this problem has yet been solved, in spite of the confidence with which ages of thousands of millions of years are ascribed to the earth and its rocks.

The lesson of Surtsey

By way of a specific example of rapid geomorphological development, we may refer to the volcanic island of Surtsey, off Iceland, which was produced during an eruption covering the period November 1963 to June 1967. Within a period of months this sterile, virgin rock was transformed into a 'mature' island with beaches, pebbles, sand, vegetation and many other features which would superficially suggest great geological age. I do not think that any radiometric dating has been carried out, but judging from such measurements made on other recent lava flows,[5] an apparent age of hundreds of millions of years might easily be obtained. I am not suggesting that Surtsey proves anything conclusively but only that the *appearance* of great age or geological maturity can be vastly misleading. The official Icelandic geologist, S. Thorarinsson writes, 'When [geologists] in the spring and summer of 1964 wandered about the island . . . they found it hard to believe that this was an island whose age was still measured in months, not years. . . . What elsewhere may take thousands of years may be accomplished [in Iceland] in one century . . .

[in] Surtsey . . . the same development may take a few weeks or even a few days.

'On Surtsey only a few months sufficed for a landscape to be created which was so varied and mature that it was almost beyond belief. . . wide sandy beaches . . . precipitous crags . . . gravel banks and lagoons, impressive cliffs grayish white from the brine . . . hollows, glens and screes . . . boulders worn by the surf, some of which were almost round on an abrasion platform cut into the cliffs.'[6]

It is clear from this evidence alone that, *given sufficiently large forces,* the rates of geomorphological development may be speeded up by orders of magnitude. The validity of the uniformitarian time-scale is thus based wholly upon the assumption that the forces acting historically within the earth's crust were, on average, those observed in today's generally quiescent conditions. If conditions such as those that shaped Surtsey prevailed to any significant extent during geological history, the age estimates may need drastic downward revision. The evidence of massive volcanism, tectonic processes, metamorphism and wholesale fossilization point to a turbulent rather than a quiescent environment over a significant portion of the earth's history.

Other evidence of a young earth

We here refer briefly to some other 'teeth marks' or evidences that the conventional geological time-scale may be excessive. None of these constitutes proof of a young earth, but equally they are just as convincing in their way as the evidence normally selected to demonstrate great geological age. We have already referred to the extremely variant ages obtained for the oceans from modern rates of accumulation of various elements. Sodium gives a geologically 'respectable' age of 260 million years, while nickel and silicon yield 8000-9000 years. Yet in his well-known undergraduate monograph 'Geological Time' my former colleague Professor J.F. Kirkaldy refers to the 'sodium age' of the oceans but not to the highly discordant data from other elements.[7]

The rate of accumulation of meteoric dust on the earth's surface is estimated at 14 million tons per year.[8] On a uniformitarian extrapolation of this figure we would expect a layer of nickel/iron some 54 feet thick to have been produced during the supposed lifetime of the earth. In fact the oceans only contain some 8000 years' worth of nickel even assuming it all came from extraterrestrial sources.

A similar calculation for the accumulation of dust on the surface of the moon led scientists to plan for the possibility that the moon landings would encounter a soft dust layer many feet in thickness. Only a few inches were in fact found. Yet moon rock is believed to be even older than the oldest terrestrial material.

It is claimed that manganese nodules on the ocean bed grow at rates indicating a vast age for the oceans. Yet sizeable nodules have been found growing as encrustations upon modern artefacts such as sparking plugs.[9] Stalactites and stalagmites have similarly been used to indicate great ages for limestone caverns, but identical structures growing at several inches per year are commonly found under bridges and other man-made constructions.

The earth's magnetic field is decaying at an observable rate. Uniformitarian extrapolation would predict that the magnetic field only 8000 years ago was equal to that of a magnetic star (this argument is not affected by reversals of the magnetic field which could occur by rotation of the poles rather than oscillations in field strength).[10]

Of course, in all these cases, the uniformitarian assumptions may be false and the calculated ages thus invalid. But what we cannot, in all fairness, do is to select as valid only those uniformitarian assumptions which give rise to ages which fit our preconceived ideas, and reject others. The only safe conclusion is that any backward extrapolation of presently observed rates is unsafe!

Radiometric dating

Radiometric dating is always quoted as final proof that the earth's crustal rocks are, in the main, millions of years old. This is not always the case, however, and a number of instances exist where tree remains embedded in 'ancient' sedimentary rock have given Carbon 14 dates of a few thousands of years.[11]

In the main, however, rocks dated by the three main radio-metric techniques (potassium-argon; the various lead series; rubidium-strontium) give ages from one million to several thousand million years (my). The basic reason why results *must* lie in these regions of time is that the age result is dominated by the half-life of the decay process employed. To clarify this statement, consider the equation for the radiometric age (t) of a rock,

$$t = 1.4 \, t_{\frac{1}{2}} \, \log_e \, (1 + D/P)$$

where $t_{\frac{1}{2}}$ is the half-life, D is the concentration of 'daughter' (radiogenic) atoms and P that of the radioactive 'parent' atom.

Of course, if $D = 0$, then $t = 0$ regardless of the half-life, but the logarithmic term varies only from 0.01 to 4.6 as the ratio D/P varies from 0.01 to 100; that is, the term multiply-ing the half-life varies only by a factor of about 500 as the D/P ratio varies by 10,000 times. Provided, therefore, that *any* daughter or parent atoms can be detected in the rock specimen (and there are practical limitations to the range of D/P ratios that can be measured reliably), the predicted rock dates are almost certain to lie in the range from one seventieth of $t_{\frac{1}{2}}$ to seven times $t_{\frac{1}{2}}$. For example, for the potassium-argon method with a half-life of 1300 my, a list[12] of 74 dates for rocks ranging from Tertiary to pre-Cambrian gave only three dates less than one-seventieth $t_{\frac{1}{2}}$ and none greater than $t_{\frac{1}{2}}$.

These considerations do not, of course, invalidate the method. But they do indicate that the ages predicted are dominated by the half-life and that the presence of *any* con-taminant or non-radiogenic 'daughter' atoms will virtually guarantee a rock age of some hundreds of millions of years.

All of this would leave radiometric dating quite unscathed *if* it could be guaranteed that no non-radiogenic daughter material were present; or that if present it could be allowed for; and that no loss or gain of either P or D atoms had occurred. Unfortunately such guarantees are not possible and the detailed literature abounds with references to just such problems, many of which are quoted by Woodmorappe.[12] Waterhouse[13] for example states, 'It is of course all too facile to "correct" various values by explanations of leakage or initially high concentrates of strontium or argon.' York and Farquhar[14] state, 'Where the results of comparisons of this sort [of different dating methods] disagree, it is clear that some sort of transfer of material into or out of the rock or mineral has taken place. It has also become apparent from the number of published discordant ages that disturbances of this nature are far more common than was formerly realized.' Again Davidson[15] writes, 'In practice very few uranium and thorium minerals have been found to exhibit this concordant pattern of ages and the much more common discordances . . . have been facilely explained away as each investigator thought best . . .'

These writers, of course, still believe in the basic validity of the dating methods and would probably argue that the majority of radiometric dates are true because they are self-consistent or agree with the stratigraphical evidence. The point I wish to make here, however, is that once one admits (as these experts do) that a significant proportion of dates are in error on account of 'contamination', material transfer, isotopic equalization ('resetting of the radiometric clock') and other hypothesized events, then the question arises as to how one differentiates an erroneous date from a true one. The answer to this question is surprising indeed, for it amounts to a calibration of the radiometric clock by the stratigraphical rates. Thus, far from the radiometric time-scale providing an 'absolute' calibration of the geological column, we find the reverse is, in practice, the case. Lest I be accused of exaggeration at this point, I offer the following quotations from the literature.

'No stratigraphic evidence is available to confirm or deny this [radiometric] age' (Wanless *et al*).[16]

'The internal consistency demonstrated above is not a sufficient test of the accuracy of the [radiometric] age determinations; they must also be consistent within any age constraints placed on intrusion by fossils in the country rocks' (Williams *et al*).[17]

'The Mississippian age for sample NS-45 cannot be correct because it is grossly inconsistent with the stratigraphic position of the lavas. No clues as to apparent preferential loss of potassium or gain of excess argon 40 from this sample are in evidence from thin section examination' (Carmichael and Palmer).[18]

'Rb-Sr analyses of an initial group of hypersthene tholeiites were well aligned on the isochron of 270 ± 45 my. This result is incorrect since it contradicts a firm stratigraphic control of the age . . .' (Compston *et al*).[19]

'In conventional interpretations of K-Ar age data it is common to discard ages which are substantially too high or too low compared with the rest of the group or with other available data such as the geological time-scale. The discrepancies . . . are arbitrarily attributed to excess or loss of argon' (Hayatsu).[20]

'. . . inherent uncertainty in dating young volcanic rocks; anomalies may be detected only by stratigraphic consistency tests, independent dating techniques and comparison with the known time-scale of geomagnetic reversals . . .' (Armstrong).[21]

In many cases, of course, there is no available stratigraphical evidence by which to check the radiometric age, this being particularly true of pre-Cambrian igneous formations. Barton[22] comments, 'As is the case with radiometric ages determined from almost any rock unit, it is impossible to establish unequivocally that the ages reported here reflect the time of original crystallization or emplacement.' Brown and Miller[23] go further: 'Much still remains to be learned of the interpretation of isotopic ages and the realization that the isotopic age is not necessarily the geological age of a rock has led to an over-sceptical attitude by some field geologists.' Such scepticism is understandable when radiometric ages are not uncommonly found to exceed the supposed age of the earth itself, for example, a plagioclase crystal dated at 4900 my,[24] a basalt with an isochron of 10 000 my,[25] and the Pharump diabase from the pre-Cambrian of California with an isochron of 34 000 my.[26] Of course, discordant results and the rejection of aberrant data are not exclusive to geology, and can be found in other branches of natural science. Enough has been said, however, to demonstrate that radiometric dating is so frequently unreliable that practising geologists insist on using the stratigraphical record (based on sedimentation rates and index fossils) to control and calibrate the radiometric clock, rather than the reverse. It is thus totally misleading to claim, as many do, that isotopic ages provide an absolute time-scale against which the standard geological column and its fossils can be checked.

These remarks apply not only to 'straightforward' techniques such as K-Ar, but also to the highly favoured isochron methods which appear at first sight to eliminate guesswork about the original isotopic constitution of the rock. All the examples cited above, where ages were obtained exceeding the supposed age of the earth, were deduced from Rb-Sr isochrons and it appears[12] that isochrons are just as likely to give geologically meaningless ages as are straightforward calculations. The present writer has studied the Rb-Sr isochron method in some detail and found that any whole rock containing two or more minerals with different initial Sr^{87}/Sr^{86} ratios must automatically give a false isochron, possibly of several hundred million years, even at zero age. The assumption that Sr^{87}/Sr^{86} ratios are identical at zero age for all closely associated minerals lies at the heart of the method and is questionable both theoretically (because of the differential mobility of the two isotopes) and experimentally (because the isotopic ratio varies widely in nature).

It will still be argued, of course, that all radiometric dates, whatever their errors, point to ages of millions of years. But these average or typical results depend on two things. Firstly, as discussed previously, we automatically factor-in ages of this magnitude by our choice of decay processes with half-lives of this order, so that *if any result is obtained at all* it is almost bound to be within two orders of magnitude of $t_{1/2}$. Secondly, we assume a zero age condition that ensures such ages. Thus in K-Ar dating (the major method used today) it is assumed that no non-radiogenic argon is present at time zero. Yet the molten magma is known to contain significant quantities of argon and indeed this fact is frequently appealed to in explaining aberrant K-Ar dates! It would be just as logical to assume some 'universal' finite concentration of argon at time zero, with a consequent reduction of predicted age. If the present atmospheric concentration of argon were taken as this universal, non-radiogenic content, K-Ar dating would give ages close to zero for most rocks.

Transcendental considerations

None of what I have written *proves* that the earth is young or *disproves* the uniformitarian approach. All I have attempted to do is to demonstrate that, on a scientific level, the question remains an open one and that to *believe* in a young earth is logically tenable.

Our options can thus be summarized as follows.

a. Accept uniformitarian ages and interpret Scripture accordingly. In the writer's view this does violence to the biblical record.

b. Adopt the view that the earth is young and that the geological evidence can legitimately be interpreted on this basis. This immediately harmonizes with the plain interpretation of Scripture.

c. Accept that geology does genuinely indicate an extended history for the earth and that Scripture does not — that is, science and Scripture do unavoidably contradict each other.

This final section is concerned with the third of these options. The question to be answered is 'Can the conflict between science and Scripture, if accepted, be resolved on a higher plane?'

The most obvious transcendental solution to the conflict lies in the theory of 'mature creation', but another possibility also exists that I will refer to as the theory of 'miraculous process'. We shall look at these in turn.

By 'mature creation' we mean the idea that the universe and its constituent parts were created with apparent ages. On this view the stars were created during the six literal days of Genesis 1, together with the wave-trains of light by which we now observe them. To the scientific observer, they genuinely appear to be billions of years old simply because they were created with that appearance. Adam was created instantly in the form of a mature grown man, with an apparent age of, say, twenty-five years, even though he did not exist the day before. Clearly, on this argument the radioactive 'clocks' used in rock-dating could have been created already 'reading' millions of years of apparently expired time.

It is obvious that 'mature creation' produces an immediate harmony between scientific observations, indicating great age, and the biblical account of a recent creation. Nothing in our scientific investigation would be capable of revealing which portion of the age of a geological feature represents true elapsed time and which portion represents an apparent age at 'time zero' (that is, creation).

Clearly, a number of objections can be raised against the doctrine of 'mature creation'. The first is the philosophical point that the same arguments can be used to assert that creation occurred at 6 a.m. this morning and that our memories of yesterday are simply part of a 'mature' creation. The force of this objection lies in the fact that such an explanation of the 'cosmos' is really no explanation at all since it does not advance our understanding of or insight into the world around us. Against this objection it can be argued that the Bible testifies *for* a mature creation some thousands of years ago. The Bible thus limits our freedom to employ any *reductio ad absurdum* to the concept of mature creation.

The second, and major, objection lies in the element of deception that some see in the idea of mature creation. Would God mislead us into thinking that rocks are millions of years old by 'planting' evidence of age in the form of partially transmuted elements? Would He create wave-trains of light between distant galaxies and earth which contained intensity variations corresponding to supernovae that never, in fact, took place? Would He confuse today's professional geologist by presenting a lithosphere consisting partly of process-generated features and partly of maturely created ones which are indistinguishable one from the other?

There is, indeed, some force in this objection, but surely not as much as is sometimes claimed. For one thing, God can hardly be charged with deception if mature creation is revealed in Scripture, as its proponents would of course claim. If men choose to ignore the Bible as a source of authoritative information, they may indeed arrive at false conclusions about the universe and its origin. But they can hardly blame God for misleading them! Secondly, even if men *are* misled by the

evidence because they insist on a rigidly naturalistic interpretation of origins, it does not follow that God *intended* to
mislead or deceive; no moral failure on His part is implied by
their fallacious thinking. Finally, there are frequent examples
in the New Testament of God 'hiding' the truth from 'the
wise and prudent' but revealing it to 'babes'.[27] The fault
again is laid fairly and squarely at the door of those whose
'minds are blinded' rather than at God's. The Christian should
surely be suspicious when men in righteous indignation accuse
God of deception!

A final objection against mature creation needs to be taken,
I think, more seriously. This is that it allows too little room
for that measure of process and duration in creation that
Scripture itself records. Mature creation is instantaneous
creation. Understood in its simplest form it requires no
process, no duration, no interactions, no labour! Yet according to Genesis, creation, and especially creation upon earth,
was a stupendous work spanning a six-day period and involving *effort* on the part of the Creator, from which in a genuine
sense He *rested* on the seventh day. I agree, of course, that
we use an anthropomorphism when we suggest that God toiled
over creation, and yet, from the brooding of the Spirit to the
forming of Eve from Adam's side, this is, indeed, the tenor of
the biblical account.

These objections to mature creation may be satisfied by
using a somewhat different perspective which I will call the
theory of 'miraculous process'. This approach shares with
mature creation the assumption that the various stages of
creation recorded in Scripture were indeed miraculous, that
is, incapable of occurring by natural process. Unlike mature
creation, however, this viewpoint recognizes explicitly that
natural law is the moment-by-moment word of God's power
by which He upholds the cosmos, and that miraculous events
occur as God changes these laws locally (in time and/or
space). I have explained this concept of the miraculous elsewhere at great length.[28]

Thus the various creative acts subsequent to the *ex nihilo*
creation itself can be regarded as manipulations of the natural
order in which events occurred, at God's command, in ways
and on time-scales inadmissible in terms of natural (that is,
normal) law.

Thus we can envisage the emergence of dry land from the primeval ocean, on day three of Genesis 1, and the gathering of the waters into seas as processes which took place much more rapidly than would be possible naturally. This could have occurred, for example, if the viscosity of water were miraculously decreased throughout the process. Similarly, the creation of living creatures 'out of the ground' suggests a rapid process of chemical combination, cell formation and growth governed and controlled by the divine Logos. This is no less miraculous, of course, than the creation of an animal, fully mature, in a 'puff of blue smoke'. It does, however, seem to the writer to be more consonant with the strong theme of process which runs through the creation narrative and more consistent with the use of existing non-living matter (the ground or the dust of the earth) as a precursor of the biosphere.

It is interesting to notice that the fixity of the fundamental laws of science is no longer accepted, even by scientists, with the assurance that it once was. In a recent issue of *New Scientist*, Dr F. Close of the Science Research Council's Rutherford Laboratory writes, 'It is crucial to our existence that the nuclear force is stronger than the electromagnetic force. If these forces had the same strength in the heat of the 'big bang', as some theories predict, then the electromagnetic force weakened, and the nuclear force strengthened as the universe cooled, yielding the forces experienced today.[29] Twenty-five years ago some cosmologists were prepared to abandon the law of the conservation of energy and matter to allow for continuous creation and thus avoid the implications of a beginning of the universe. The idea that miraculously accelerated processes played a part in the history of the universe can thus not be dismissed as inadmissible, even from a strictly scientific viewpoint. Dr Close's statement, for example, bears directly upon the question of historical radioactive decay rates since these are intimately associated with the 'nuclear force'. A strengthening nuclear force during cosmological history would be expected to result in a slowing down of nuclear decay rates and a corresponding exaggeration of ages calculated from current nuclear half-lives.

Conclusion

We conclude that uniformitarian geology is based upon a less secure scientific foundation than is normally admitted. Radiometric dating is far more problematical than most people appreciate and the old geological column (based upon arbitrary sedimentation rates) remains the touchstone of geological time. This time-scale is, on scientific considerations alone, likely to be greatly exaggerated.

Although, therefore, the uniformitarian approach is the simplest, it is scientifically insecure. The facts of observation are equally consistent with a 'young earth' interpretation.

The main failing, however, of uniformitarian geology is that it refuses to admit the biblical testimony that miraculous process was operative during the formation of the universe and the earth. Recent scientific thinking, though speculative, admits that even the basic laws of physics may not be immutable in time. If this line of thinking is ever confirmed it would provide independent evidence of miraculous (that is, non-contemporary) process in nature.

References

1. Young, D.A., *Creation and the flood,* Baker Book House, Grand Rapids, 1977, pp.76-78.
2. De Young, D.B., 'The precision of nuclear decay rates', *Creation Research Society Quarterly 13,* No.1, 1976, pp.38-41.
3. Andrews, E.H., *From nothing to nature,* Evangelical Press, Welwyn, 1978, pp.60-63.
4. Morris, H.M., cited by Monty White, A.J., *What about origins?,* Dunestone Printers, Newton Abbot, 1978, pp.128-129.
5. Clementson, S.P., *Creation Res. Soc. Quarterly 7,* 1970, p.137.
6. Thorarinsson, S., *Surtsey: the new island in the N. Atlantic,* Viking Press, N.Y., 1967, pp.39-40. See also *Creation Res. Soc. Quarterly 16,* No.1, 1979, pp.3-7.

7. Kirkaldy, J.F., *Geological time,* Oliver & Boyd, Edinburgh, 1971, pp.46-48.
8. Petterson, H., *Scientific American 202,* 1960, p.132.
9. Lewis, E.J., 'Tapping the world's deepest wettest mine', *Popular Mechanics, 150,* No.5, p.91.
10. Barnes, T.G., *Origin and destiny of the earth's magnetic field,* Tech. Monograph No.3, Institute for Creation Research, Creation-Life Publishers, San Diego, 1973.
11. Beierle, F.P., *Creation Res. Soc. Quarterly 16,* No.2, 1979, p.87.
12. Woodmorappe, J., 'Radiometric geochronology reappraised', *Creation Res. Soc. Quarterly 16,* No.2, 1979, p.102.
13. Waterhouse, J.B., in *Contributions to the geologic time scale,* Amer. Assn. of Petroleum Geologists, Studies in Geology No.6, 1978, p.316.
14. York, D. and Farquhar, R.M., *The earth's age and geochronology,* Pergamon Press, Oxford, 1972.
15. Davidson, C.F., 'Some aspects of radiogeology', *Liverpool Manchester Geological J., 2,* 1960, p.314.
16. Wanless, R.K. *et al, Geological Survey of Canada Paper,* 69-2A, 1970, p.24.
17. Williams, I.S. *et al, J. Geolog. Soc. Australia 22,* (4), 1975, p.502.
18. Carmichael, C.M. and Palmer, H.C., *J. Geophysical Res. 73,* 1968, p.2813.
19. Compston, W. *et al, Geochimica et Cosmochimica Acta, 32,* p.131.
20. Hayatsu, A., *Canadian J. of Earth Sci. 16,* 1979, p.974.
21. Armstrong, B.L., *New Zealand J. Geol. & Geophys. 21,* 1978, p.692.
22. Barton, J.M. Jr., *Canadian J. of Earth Sci., 14,* 1977, p.1641.
23. Brown, P.E. and Miller, J.A., *Quarterly J. Geol. Soc. Lond.,* Special Publn. No.3, *Time and Place in Orogeny,* 1969, p.137.
24. *The Phanerozoic Time Scale,* Geol. Soc. Lond. Special Publn. 120s, 1964, pp.377-8.

25. Mark, R.K. *et al, Geol. Soc. Amer. Abstracts with Programs 6,* 1974, p.456.
26. Woodmorappe, J., *op. cit.,* p.122.
27. Matthew 11:25.
28. Andrews, E.H., *op. cit.,* pp.101-104.
29. Close, F., *New Scientist,* 29 November 1979.

Other titles by Prof. Andrews published by Evangelical Press

Is Evolution Scientific?

The theory of evolution is all but universally accepted in the Western world today as an explanation of the origin of life. Claiming support from a variety of sciences, those who press the claims of evolution assert that the matter is "scientifically proven as far as events not witnessed by man can ever be".

There are, however, scientists of various disciplines who maintain that many aspects of the theory of evolution offend the canons of rigorous science. They recognize that the mechanisms by which the evolution of life and biological species is said to have occurred are, at best, unproven hypotheses and, at worst, contradictions of the experimental facts. Professor Andrews is one such scientist. In this book he examines the nature of genuine scientific theory and applies the principles so established to the theory of evolution to see whether it does, in fact, pass muster as "scientific" in the best sense of the word.

From Nothing to Nature

The theory of evolution continues to be taught in most schools and colleges as a proven fact. There is, however, a growing number of scientists who are questioning this theory. One such scientist is the author of this book. Writing in an easy-to-understand manner, he gives scientific and biblical answers to such questions as: "Where did we come from?", "How did life begin?", and "How old is the earth?"

Although written mainly for the younger reader, *From Nothing to Nature* will be appreciated by all, particularly by those who have little or no scientific background. Prof. Andrews does not apologise for accepting the Genesis account of creation. After reading this book, neither will you!